MURRAY

MURRAY

JOHN MURRAY

DINO

Published by Dino Books
an imprint of John Blake Publishing
3 Bramber Court, 2 Bramber Road,
London W14 9PB, England

www.johnblakebooks.com

www.facebook.com/johnblakebooks f
twitter.com/jblakebooks t

This edition published in 2017

ISBN: 978 1 78 606 468 4

British Library Cataloguing-in-Publication Data:

A catalogue record for this book is available from the British Library.

Design by www.envydesign.co.uk
Cover illustration by Dan Leydon
Background image: Shutterstock

Printed in Great Britain by CPI Group (UK) Ltd

1 3 5 7 9 10 8 6 4 2

Papers used by John Blake Publishing are natural, recyclable products made from
wood grown in sustainable forests. The manufacturing processes conform to the
environmental regulations of the country of origin.

Every attempt has been made to contact the relevant copyright-holders, but some
were unobtainable. We would be grateful if the appropriate people could contact us.

John Blake Publishing is an imprint of Bonnier Publishing.
www.bonnierpublishing.com

For Clare and Beth

TABLE OF CONTENTS

CHAPTER 1

TOP OF THE WORLD

As the two players walked on to the court, they were greeted by an ear-splitting roar. Floodlights flashed, smoke filled the arena and the crowd – all 17,000 of them – rose to their feet to show their support.

It was a fitting atmosphere for the last and most important match of the 2016 tennis season. The next few hours would decide who would finish the year with the precious world No. 1 ranking.

On one side of the court was Novak Djokovic, the defending champion from Serbia and the world's best player for the previous three years. On the other side was the challenger – Britain's Andy Murray – bidding for his first ATP World Tour Finals title, in front of his home crowd in London.

'Wow,' Andy said to himself as he looked around the packed O2 Arena. 'I hope I can give everyone a match to remember.'

He looked up to the stands where his coaching team were sitting with his wife Kim and mum Judy. He waved to Kim.

'Come on, Andy,' Kim shouted in support.

It always gave Andy confidence to know his family was cheering him on. Of course, he was nervous ahead of such a big match, but there were plenty of reasons to be positive.

Andy had enjoyed his best ever season in 2016. He had won the Wimbledon title for the second time. He had won an Olympic gold medal, also for the second time. And he came into this match on the back of twenty-three wins in a row.

Two weeks earlier, he had claimed the world No. 1 ranking for the first ever time after winning a tournament in Paris. That ended Novak's run of 122 weeks at the top.

Now, if he could win one more match, he would finish the year as world No. 1. But if he lost, Novak would grab the title back off him.

Andy's coach, Ivan Lendl, caught his attention above the deafening noise of the crowd. 'You can do this, Andy. Go out there, treat it like any other game and you'll be fine.'

Andy smiled. It was great to have someone with so much tennis experience on his team. If anyone knew what it took to be the world's top player, it was Ivan; at one point in his tennis career, from 1985, he had held the No. 1 ranking for an incredible 157 weeks in a row.

'I'll be happy with just one more week,' Andy thought as he walked to the net to meet Novak for the coin toss. The pair shook hands.

'Good luck, Andy,' Novak said.

'Good luck to you too, Novak,' Andy replied. 'May the best man win.'

'Let's hope that means me today!' Novak laughed.

While the two players had built up a strong rivalry on the professional tennis circuit, they remained good friends. In fact, their friendship went all the way back to when they were juniors. Born within one week of each other, they used to practise together growing up and also compete on the junior circuit.

But now it was time for Andy to put any feelings of friendship aside and get down to business.

'Let's go, Andy, let's go,' the crowd chanted in unison.

After winning the toss, Andy got the match underway… and promptly served a double fault to hand Novak the first point. The crowd groaned.

'Well, it can't get any worse than that,' Andy said to himself. He took a deep breath and remembered Ivan's advice. 'Treat it like any other game.'

With those words running around his head, he quickly settled and won the game to calm any nerves.

Leading 4–3, Andy had his first sniff of a chance to break Novak's serve. A pile-driving forehand forced his opponent to hit a backhand into the net, opening up a 5–3 lead.

One game later, the home favourite wrapped up the opening set thanks to some stunning hitting. Kim and the rest of the crowd leapt to their feet to applaud.

'Just one more set, Andy,' screamed Kim.

Andy had been worried that he might be feeling tired after his efforts in the previous day's semi-final. He had eventually beaten Canada's Milos Raonic in an unforgettable match that lasted three hours and thirty-eight minutes, the longest ever in the tournament's history.

However, he showed no signs of fatigue against Novak as he continued to hit top form in the second set. He quickly opened up a 4–1 lead before his opponent fought back like a true champion. Eventually, after a titanic tussle, Andy had the chance to serve for the match, and his place in history.

The first two match points came and went.

'Third time lucky, Andy,' Kim yelled.

As was often the case, Kim was right. One booming serve later, Andy was the champion.

He dropped his racket and threw his cap to the

ground before pumping his fist with joy. He had become the seventeenth player to finish the year as the world's top player and the first Briton to do so since the computer rankings system had been introduced.

The battle over, the two friends shared a warm embrace at the net.

'Well played, Novak,' said Andy.

'Well done, Andy. You deserve it,' Novak replied. 'But I'll be back again next year to fight for my number 1 ranking.'

The stadium announcer had a special message for the crowd: 'Ladies and gentlemen, put your hands together for the ATP World Tour Finals champion and new world number one – Andy Murray.'

And no one cheered more loudly than Kim: 'You're my number one, Andy!'

Later, as Andy sat in the dressing room with his coaching team, he received a text message on his phone. It was from his brother Jamie: 'Welcome to the club.'

'Just like Jamie to keep my feet on the ground,'

Andy chuckled. Earlier that week, his brother had sealed his own special place in history, finishing the year as the world's No. 1 ranked doubles player.

Andy and Jamie were on top of the tennis world. Not a bad effort from two brothers from a small Scottish town of fewer than 10,000 people.

CHAPTER 2

A BORN NATURAL

'Out.'

'What do you mean, "out"? The ball clearly hit the line.'

'Rubbish. It was so far out it was nearly in the other court.'

From the moment he first picked up a racket, Andy was extremely competitive on the tennis court. And when his older brother Jamie was the player on the other side of the net, there were, unsurprisingly, no shortage of arguments – much to the frustration of their parents Judy and Will.

'Whatever happened to brotherly love?' Judy would often say as she tried to split up yet another squabble.

Growing up in Dunblane – an hour north of the Scottish capital Edinburgh – Andy was always keen to beat Jamie, whatever they were playing, be it a board game, re-enacting wrestling bouts from the TV or kicking a football around the garden.

Football was Andy's favourite sport, and he loved nothing more than watching his team Hibernian play, for whom his grandfather Roy had once been a player. But it was Judy who suggested that he take up tennis.

His mum had been a very handy player herself and thought it would be a good idea for her sons to try out the sport at the local courts – and burn off some excess energy in the process.

One day, Judy decided it was time for the boys to play their first match.

'Jamie, why don't you turn the wrestling off and take Andy with you to the tennis court?'

'Sure,' replied Jamie, 'but only if Andy is happy to lose!'

'We'll see about that,' said Andy.

Two hours later, the door to the family home –

which was just around the corner from the courts –
crashed open, followed by Jamie, then a racket flung
to the floor, and finally one very angry-looking Andy.

'*Champione, champione, ole, ole, ole,*' came the
winning chant from Jamie.

'I definitely would have won if the sun hadn't
been in my eyes when I was serving,' grumbled
Andy. 'And I'm sure my forehand in the last game
landed in.'

'No one likes a sore loser,' laughed Judy as she
stroked her younger son's head. 'But apart from the
result, did you enjoy the game?'

'I suppose it was okay,' Andy conceded quietly,
'although I'm not sure if it's as much fun as football.'
He added: 'Jamie might be fifteen months older than
me, but I'll beat him next time.'

'Well, next time I'll come along with you too and
might even give you a few tips on how to beat your
brother,' Judy promised.

After finishing her career as a player, Judy had
been determined to stay involved in tennis and so
took up coaching. She encouraged her sons to play as

much as possible – when the famously unpredictable Scottish weather allowed – and was always on hand to deliver some useful advice.

'Keep your eye on the ball.'

'Make sure you move your feet.'

'Don't hit the ball directly at Jamie!'

While Andy didn't manage to beat his brother on that next occasion, he improved each time he stepped on to the court. Before long, his weekends were no longer devoted to watching Hibs and scoring goals for his local football team, but to tennis instead. And that regularly meant long drives to tournaments in towns all over Scotland.

'Are you confident today?' Judy asked Andy, as the minibus set off on another early Saturday morning trip. Her role as coach frequently doubled up with driving duties, as she willingly gave up her weekends to take Andy, Jamie and other young players to various competitions around the country.

'I think it will be tough, Mum,' Andy replied. 'A lot of the players are a few years older than me.' He gazed out of the misty window, wondering how he could get the better of players almost twice his size.

Yet more often than not, Andy would prove that he was more than a match for the older, bigger players. Come the drive home, there would regularly be one extra 'passenger' in the minibus – the winner's trophy.

'*Champione, champione, ole, ole, ole,*' Andy sang in the back seat, as he lifted his trophy in the air, imagining doing the same thing one day on Wimbledon's famous Centre Court.

'You might have beaten the older boys in Dumfries, but you still can't beat me,' Jamie teased.

'We'll see about that,' came the swift reply.

CHAPTER 3

FIGHTING SPIRIT

'This is it. Match point for Andre Agassi. He has come from two sets down in the French Open final against Andrei Medvedev to stand on the brink of history.'

'A big serve from Agassi, Medvedev's return is long, and that's it – he's done it. The American superstar has become only the fifth player in history to win all four Grand Slam titles!'

Andy leapt in the air and raised his arms to the skies. He was imagining that he was his hero Andre Agassi, forgetting for a moment that he was supposed to be sitting quietly in the classroom concentrating on a maths test. His schoolmates giggled as Andy received a telling off from the teacher.

'Typical Andy, always thinking about tennis.'

'The only time he focuses on maths is when he's counting the number of points he's won in a match!'

As his passion for tennis grew, Andy spent a lot more time thinking about the sport – much to his mum's annoyance when it came at the expense of his schoolwork.

'Please can you concentrate on algebra and arithmetic today, not Andre Agassi,' Judy said as she waved Andy off to school.

'Sorry Mum, I do *want* to learn… but to learn how to hit a smash as hard as Pete Sampras, how to serve faster than a high-speed train like Goran Ivanišević, and how to return every ball on the court just like Andre does.'

As important as Andy's schoolwork was, deep down Judy knew that she couldn't stand in his way as he chased his tennis dream. The more he played, the more he won and the more tournaments he entered – and that meant much more driving on the weekends for his mum. They travelled all over Great Britain – around Scotland, down to London, even to Wales. With Jamie also in the back of the minibus, the journeys would rarely be quiet, particularly if the brothers were playing in the same event.

One day, the brothers were having another squabble as they drove down to Solihull in the Midlands for an under-10s tournament.

'We're here!' shouted Andy as the minibus pulled into the tennis centre car park. 'I can't wait for this competition.'

'Don't get too excited. You'll have to beat me first if you want to get your hands on the trophy,' replied Jamie, giving his brother a friendly dig in the ribs.

This tournament was different, however: Andy and Jamie would meet in the final. And this time, Andy would be victorious.

'Game, set and match, Murray,' announced the umpire as Andy won the final deciding point.

'You mean "Game, set and match, *Andy* Murray!"' shouted Andy as he ran to meet his dejected brother at the net.

After waiting so many years to beat his older

brother, Andy could not contain his delight. And he let Jamie know about it all the way home.

'How does it feel to lose to your little brother?' Andy teased.

'Would you two boys behave yourselves please?' Judy pleaded from the front of the minibus. 'I'd like to get us all home safely.'

Her words fell on deaf ears.

'It must really hurt to be on the losing side of the net.'

Finally, Jamie had suffered enough. 'Losing hurts a lot – but not as much as this,' he replied, thumping his brother's hand that was resting on the seat.

'Aaarrrggghhh, my finger!' Andy screamed in pain.

Judy quickly pulled the minibus over to the side of the road to see what all the noise was about. She opened the door to find Andy in tears, with lots of blood … and without a fingernail. Jamie had hit Andy so hard that his nail had come off.

'What on earth is going on back here?' Judy asked while shaking her head, as Jamie sat sheepishly in his seat. 'Right, it's off to the doctor for you, Andy.'

A few days later, when all the commotion had finally died down and the doctor had patched up Andy's finger, Judy gave the boys a stern talking-to.

'Jamie, you must never hit your brother in any circumstances – whatever he has said to you. And Andy, you have to learn to be modest in victory.'

While Judy knew her sons needed to focus their aggression on hitting tennis balls instead of each other, she was also secretly proud that they showed such fighting spirit. That would help them enormously if they wanted to be top tennis players one day.

When Andy was eleven years old, Judy made another decision that would make him a better player – she hired a coach for him. Up to that point, Judy had looked after the main coaching duties for Andy, but she knew how important it was to get some expert advice.

'Hi Andy, my name is Leon.'

'Pleased to meet you, Leon. I'm really looking forward to learning as much as possible from you.'

Little did Andy know at the time, but nearly twenty years later he would be on the same team as Leon Smith.

For now, though, there were more important things to concentrate on – such as winning tournaments. For Andy, tournaments didn't come any bigger than the Junior Orange Bowl in Miami, USA.

'I'm going to America!' he shouted, running around the house after ripping open his invitation. 'That's where so many of the greatest ever tennis players have come from – John McEnroe, Chris Evert, Sampras and, of course, Andre.'

Being invited to the tournament was a huge honour – the competition was for the best players in the world under the age of twelve. Andy was joined on the trip to Miami by Judy and his gran.

'I hope you're not scared of flying, Mum,' he laughed as the plane soared into the skies.

'Anything is better than driving you in a minibus!'

Once they arrived in America, Andy proved he was just as good at playing on foreign soil as at home. He advanced all the way to the final, where he saved his best for the match against Tomas Piskacek from the Czech Republic.

'Well played, Tomas. You had a great tournament,' Andy said warmly to his beaten opponent after the match.

'I'm sure we'll be hearing lots more about you in years to come,' Tomas replied.

'That's my boy,' screamed Judy as Andy collected the winner's trophy.

'That's my grandson!' shouted his gran.

'I'd love to come back to America one day and play in all the big senior tournaments,' Andy thought as he clutched the trophy, which in fact was a big Orange Bowl.

Later on, when they left the tournament and headed to the airport for the long journey home, Andy handed over the trophy to his gran.

'Here you go, gran. This is to say thank you for coming all this way to support me. It means a lot to have such great support. And if there's no room on your mantelpiece, you can use the bowl for a fruit salad at Christmas.'

'Ah, thanks Andy. That's exactly what we'll do. You can't beat the taste of success!'

CHAPTER 4

VIVA ESPAÑA

While things were going well for Andy on the court, everything was about to change in his life at home.

A few years earlier, his parents Judy and Will had separated – which had been very hard for Andy and Jamie – and now there was another major upheaval around the corner.

'Andy, we've decided that if you want to become the best tennis player you can be,' Judy explained, 'then you need the best possible training… and so we think you should move to Barcelona.'

'Barcelona? I thought you said "best tennis player", not "footballer",' Andy replied with a puzzled look.

Although tennis was his main obsession these days, he still keenly followed football. Like many fans of his age, he was in awe of FC Barcelona and the wonderful players from all over the world who graced the famous team.

Judy smiled. 'Spain has its fair share of famous tennis players too. There is a school in Barcelona called the Sánchez-Casal Academy, which has trained some of the greatest players to have picked up a racket, including the multiple Grand Slam champion Martina Hingis.'

'It will really help your development to practise every day with older players,' added Leon, 'and to be taught by some of the best tennis brains in the business. The courts in Barcelona are made of clay, which means the ball bounces higher and travels more slowly. You will have the opportunity to learn how to play on a different surface, which is what the very best players must do.'

'Plus the weather is great, so you will be able to play every day of the week, rather than sitting inside in Scotland waiting for the rain to stop,' said Judy.

'So, what do you think?'

Andy sat in silence for a few minutes. He knew it would be a great opportunity and could help him achieve his dream of becoming a top tennis player. But it would be hard to say goodbye to everything and everyone he knew so well in Dunblane – the local tennis courts, his grandparents who lived only a few minutes away, his parents and, of course, Jamie.

Everyone was waiting with bated breath. Finally, he looked up.

'Okay, I'll do it,' he said. 'Especially if it means I don't have to go to school anymore!'

'Oh, you'll still have to do that,' laughed Judy. 'There will still be plenty of time for studying in between tennis training.'

Later that week, when Jamie was helping him to pack his suitcase, Andy chatted about moving away from home.

'I know we're constantly travelling to tennis tournaments,' said Andy, 'but we've always known we would come home at the end of them. This will be different. I'll miss you all a lot.'

'Don't worry,' replied Jamie. 'I'm sure you'll forget all about us as soon as you start messing around on the beach with your new friends.'

'There won't be any time for sunbathing,' Andy laughed, 'but at least it will give you a chance to win some tournaments at home without me around to stop you.'

Jamie grinned. Ever since the 'Solihull squabble', Andy had been a much more gracious winner besides, he would need all his fingers intact if he was to become a success in Spain.

And so it was, in September 2002, at the age of fifteen, that the curly-haired teenager Andy waved goodbye to the small Scottish town of Dunblane and said hello to the next stage of his life in a city of 1.5 million people: Barcelona.

On arriving at the academy, Andy was shown around the dormitory where he would sleep with the other boys and was introduced to some of his dormmates.

'Hi, I'm Dani, from Venezuela. This is Juan – he's Argentinian. And this is Carlos – he's from Peru.'

'Pleased to meet you. My name's Andy. I'm from Dunblane in Scotland.' He thought his hometown sounded very boring in comparison to those exotic countries.

'You'd better get some rest, Andy,' said Dani, putting his arm around his new friend's shoulder. 'Your first practice session is tomorrow and you've got an extremely tough opponent.'

'Really? Who's that then?' Andy asked, looking nervously around the dorm.

'Me!' Dani shouted, as everyone in the room burst into laughter.

The next morning at practice, Andy made an instant impression.

'Great hitting, Andy. They must have taught you well in Dunblane.'

'Thanks Dani. I really enjoyed it, but there is one thing that is worrying me.'

'What's that?'

'We're in Spain, all the coaches are from Spain, and I don't speak any Spanish, so how am I going to learn anything?'

Dani chuckled. 'No need to worry. Everyone speaks English here.'

'Phew. That's a relief. I could try to learn the language, but my mum will tell you I'm not the best pupil!'

Andy quickly settled into life in Spain. He played more tennis each day than he had ever thought possible – and still had to find time to fit in his schoolwork. The more he played, the better his game and strokes developed. The hot weather was a shock to the system but being forced to run around in the heat made Andy a lot fitter.

'Playing in such high temperatures will really help me if I ever become a professional, when you have to compete in different climates all over the world,' he thought.

As part of his training, he regularly travelled around Europe to take part in tournaments against the best players on the Continent.

'We're so lucky to visit all these famous cities,' Andy said to Dani.

'There's no chance to do any sightseeing, though, as all we do is play tennis,' grumbled Dani.

'Well, you'll have to make sure you get knocked out of the tournament early, then you'll have plenty of time on your hands,' joked Andy.

One week, Andy was competing in a tournament in France. His opponent was a player from Serbia called Novak Djokovic. Like Andy, Novak had also moved away from his home country to a tennis school in Munich, Germany, and was making a name for himself on the junior circuit.

Andy won the match, but he didn't need to have a coaching certificate at his academy to know that he had come up against a very classy opponent. He thought it wouldn't be long before they would face each other again.

'See you again soon, Novak,' he said after the match.

'Hopefully the result will be different next time,' Novak smiled.

CHAPTER 5

A BRIGHT FUTURE

By the end of his time at the Sánchez-Casal Academy, Andy was ready to take the next step in his tennis journey. For eighteen months, he had completely dedicated himself to the sport – playing, listening, learning, and then playing some more.

He had impressed his coaches with his attitude off the court, too. Never tempted to stay out late partying, he would spend any free time watching DVDs with Dani, Carlos and other friends, or going to see the latest film at Barcelona's English language cinema – when he wasn't catching up on sleep, that was.

The only setback came in 2003 when Andy

injured his right knee. He had to return home to Dunblane for several months to rest. Being a very energetic person, used to playing five to six hours of tennis every day, that proved quite challenging.

'Jamie, can't I just join you on the court for a few rallies?' he begged his brother.

'No chance. If you don't rest your knee, you could do some permanent damage to it – and then you'll never be able to beat me again.'

'I could beat you standing on one leg!'

Luckily, Andy listened to his brother's advice and later that year, when his knee was fully healed, he was ready to resume doing what he loved best – competing in, and winning, tournaments. That's exactly what the brothers did when they teamed up to win the Scottish International Doubles.

'It feels strange to be playing on the same side of the net,' said Jamie as the brothers held up the trophy together after the final.

'At least we won't have to argue on the way home about this match,' Andy grinned.

Winning tournaments was about to get a lot

harder, however. As well as entering the elite junior events, Andy had been advised by his coaches to dip his toe into the choppy waters of the senior circuit. He was sixteen and was about to compete against players who were twice his age, or even older, and had far more experience.

'This will be my toughest test yet,' a worried Andy said to Dani one evening. 'But it will be a great opportunity to challenge myself against the best and see what it takes to become a true champion.'

'You're definitely ready for this, Andy,' Dani reassured his friend. 'Besides, Boris Becker won Wimbledon aged seventeen, so you'd better get a move on if you're going to beat his record!'

Much as Andy would have loved to emulate the great German player, his Wimbledon dream would have to wait for now. In order even to qualify for Wimbledon, which was the most famous tennis tournament in the world, Andy needed to be ranked in the top 100 players in the men's game. While his junior ranking had climbed to a high of No. 6, it was a different story in the official ATP World Rankings.

At the time of the 2003 Wimbledon tournament, he was ranked No. 774.

'Only about another 700 places to go!' Andy chuckled to himself.

Putting thoughts of Wimbledon glory to one side, he began to focus on the lower-level Futures and Challenger tournaments, which offered the opportunity to build ranking points if he did well. While Andy was impatient to take on the world's best players in the top competitions, his coach Leon reminded him how important these events were for his development.

'Everyone has to start somewhere. Remember, there are no easy matches on the men's tennis tour, whoever you're playing.'

'Let's just hope Futures stands for future champion!' Andy said.

He didn't have to wait long to get his hands on his first trophy. A couple of months after making his senior debut in the Manchester Challenger event, he travelled to Glasgow for a Futures tournament.

'It feels great to be back in Scotland, Mum.'

'Let's hope you can give the home fans something to cheer about,' Judy replied.

Andy read the script perfectly. In the city where he had been born sixteen years earlier, he drew on all the lessons he had learned in Spain, competing against older and more experienced players, and won his first Futures event. He was the youngest ever British player to win a senior tournament.

As Andy paraded the trophy to the Scottish supporters in the stands, the event organiser walked over and handed him an envelope.

'What's this? I'm not in trouble, am I?' asked Andy, casting his mind back to the days when his schoolteacher had made him take scolding letters home to his parents.

'Open it and see,' laughed the organiser.

'A sum of $1,300 made payable to… Andy Murray,' he read in disbelief. The winner's cheque might not have been an enormous sum compared to what the best players earned each week, but for Andy it was a small fortune.

'Spend it wisely,' Judy said later as she

congratulated her son. 'That's enough to buy a new tennis racket, shoes and clothes.'

'And still have enough left to buy a couple of video games,' Andy added with a grin.

CHAPTER 6

IN THE SPOTLIGHT

'Wait a minute. Isn't that David Beckham?'

'There goes the boxer Joe Calzaghe.'

'And Kelly Holmes is right behind by him. She won double Olympic gold in Athens.'

Andy could not contain his excitement. Everywhere he looked there was another British sporting superstar standing a few metres away.

He was at the BBC Television Centre in London for the 2004 Sports Personality of the Year awards. He had been invited to the glitzy ceremony as he was shortlisted for the Young Personality of the Year award, and he felt like the luckiest sports fan alive – never in his life had he been so close to so many heroes.

'I'm sure if you ask nicely they'll be happy to pose for a photo,' said Judy, who was accompanying her son to the event.

'No chance! They won't know who I am.'

'Remember, son. You deserve to be here just as much as anyone else.'

Andy had enjoyed a tremendous 2004 season, establishing himself as one of the stars of the Futures circuit. He won three titles in Spain and another in Italy, with an overall tally of twenty-six wins and just three defeats. Andy was starting to show the experience and tactical knowledge he would need to compete with the senior players.

The highlight of his season had actually come at a junior competition. Not just any junior competition, but the Junior US Open – one of the four Grand Slam tournaments that are the biggest events on the tennis calendar.

'Greats of the games like Roger Federer, Stefan Edberg and Andy Roddick have all won junior Grand Slam titles,' Dani told his friend on the eve of the tournament, 'and look what they have achieved at senior level.'

'No pressure then,' Andy grimaced, as he thought about the jump in class to the Swiss superstar Federer, who had won three senior Grand Slam events in 2004 alone.

Leon Smith would not be at Andy's side to guide him through the tournament, though. They had decided that it was the right time to move on after many successful years together.

'Thanks for everything, Leon. I've learned so much from you and wouldn't be where I am now if it wasn't for your help.'

'You'll be just fine without me, Andy,' Leon replied. 'But if you ever need any advice or want to chat about anything – tennis, football, girlfriend problems, whatever! – don't hesitate to pick up the phone.'

As it turned out, Leon was absolutely right. Andy might have been over 3,000 miles away from home, but he showed no signs of nerves – he was as settled in New York as the Statue of Liberty. He beat a string of top opponents on the way to the final, including Argentina's Juan Martín del Potro and local favourite Sam Querrey.

His devastating form continued in the final as he brushed aside Sergiy Stakhovsky, from Ukraine, to seal the title. The new champion had dropped just one set along the way – in football terms, that's the equivalent of conceding only one goal in the whole World Cup.

The win was the perfect way to ease the pain from two days earlier when Andy and Jamie had lost in the semi-finals of the doubles.

'I'm sorry that we don't have another trophy to add to this one,' Andy apologised to his brother.

'Forget about it. Let's hope we both have a chance to go for the senior title here one day.'

When he arrived back in Scotland, Andy realised that life as he knew it would never be the same. The curly-haired kid from Dunblane had caught the attention of the national press and was being billed as the most promising junior player Britain had produced in years.

'No pressure then,' Andy thought again.

TV interviews and newspaper articles quickly followed and, not long after, the invitation to the Sports Personality of the Year awards arrived through the letterbox.

On the day of the ceremony, Andy was a bag of nerves as he got ready in his hotel room. He used to watch the awards on TV every Christmas with Jamie, arguing over who they thought would win each prize. Now he would be watching the ceremony a few rows back from the main stage where hosts Gary Lineker and Sue Barker were standing.

'Best go to the loo one more time just in case,' he mumbled nervously, closing the toilet door behind him.

But when he went to open the door again, the lock wouldn't turn. He tried and tried – pushing, pulling, knocking and hitting; it wouldn't budge.

At first he remained calm.

'Don't worry, it's a busy hotel. Someone will come soon and let you out,' he thought.

Then he started to panic.

'It's ruined. My one chance to meet my sporting idols face to face, and I'll have to spend the evening stuck on the loo.'

And finally he got desperate.

'Heeelllppp!'

Luckily, after what seemed like an eternity – and a lot more fretting – Andy managed to break free from the toilet just in the nick of time.

'Come on, we're going to miss the start,' Judy said as she rushed out of the hotel with her flustered-looking son. 'What took you so long anyway?'

'Let's just say I had a wee bit of trouble, but I'm okay now!'

And he was more than just okay a couple of hours later when Sue Barker – a very familiar face to Andy from all the years she had presented the BBC's tennis coverage – read out the result.

'And the winner of the BBC Young Sports Personality of the Year award for making giant strides in the world of tennis in the past twelve months, during which time he won the US Open junior title is… Andy Murray.'

Once again, Andy was in a state of disbelief. 'What an incredible day,' he said to himself as he was ushered up to the stage to be presented with the award.

By now, he was used to winning trophies, but only on a tennis court and often in front of a few hundred people. This was something different entirely – in front of a national TV audience, flashing lights and more camera lenses than he could count.

As he looked at the names engraved on the prized trophy, the co-host Gary Lineker leaned over and said: 'You're in esteemed company, Andy. Some of Britain's best athletes have won this award, including Wayne Rooney a couple of years ago. He's now one of the best footballers on the planet.'

'No pressure then, Gary,' Andy laughed.

CHAPTER 7

WELCOME TO WIMBLEDON

Andy stared intently at the computer screen. He scanned the list of names in front of him.

'Come on, it must be somewhere…'

He looked further and further down the page before finally stopping with a shout.

'Found it. Four hundred and seven.'

'What's that?' Jamie asked with a twinkle in his eye. 'The number of times you've lost to me at tennis?'

Andy gave his brother a friendly shove. 'It's my world ranking. And my new year's resolution for 2005 is to reach the top hundred by the end of the season.'

Judy smiled as she watched her two sons teasing

each other. While they still enjoyed messing around together like kids at home, they had grown from boys to men on the tennis court and were now ready to take on the seniors – Andy in the singles events, Jamie on the doubles circuit.

'If you want to be in the world's top hundred, then it's time for you to turn professional, Andy,' Judy explained. 'Are you ready to be a full-time tennis player?'

The answer came back faster than a backhand smash. 'Absolutely!'

Decision made, the next few months were a whirlwind of firsts for Andy as he made his first strides as a professional tennis player. As well as playing tournaments week in, week out, he became the youngest ever player to represent Great Britain in the Davis Cup, helping his country win the tie against Israel with victory in his doubles match.

'I know tennis is an individual sport, but it feels great to be part of a team,' said Andy, who had once dreamed of playing football for Scotland in the World Cup.

'Especially when it's a winning team,' his doubles partner David Sherwood added.

In April, Andy made his first-ever appearance in an ATP World Tour event – a significant step up from the Futures and Challenger tournaments. After taking the first set from Czech opponent Jan Hernych, he couldn't hold his lead and lost in three close sets.

'That was a terrible performance,' Andy complained to Judy afterwards.

'Andy, I know it doesn't mean much right now, but you should be very proud. You nearly beat a player who is ranked number seventy-nine in the world and is eight years older than you.'

Andy nodded. He knew that he could be very hard on himself, but he really wanted to do whatever it took to reach the top.

As the professional tennis tour rolled into London in the summer of 2005, two crucial things happened that would help Andy in his bid to achieve his goal. First, former British Davis Cup player Mark Petchey became Andy's coach. The pair hit it off instantly, having a laugh together off the court while also knowing when it was time to be serious and get down to business. Wimbledon was fast approaching and Andy was desperately hoping he could play in the men's event.

'What's it like to play in the Wimbledon senior draw, Petch?' Andy asked his coach, who had been a regular at the All England Club during his playing career.

'Andy, as much as I enjoy coaching, I would give anything to play on those famous grass courts one last time.'

Andy listened spellbound as Petch relived his best Wimbledon performance in 1997 when – cheered on by a raucous British crowd – he had progressed to the third round before losing to the great Boris Becker.

'Wow. I would give anything even to play just once in the men's event!'

A few weeks later, the Wimbledon organisers made Andy's dream come true. In recognition of the tremendous progress he had made on tour, they gave him a wildcard into the main draw.

As part of his preparations, he got a taste of what it was like to play in front of a home crowd in London at the Queen's Club Championships. In a sign of his ever-improving tennis brain, Andy quickly mastered the grass-court conditions – with their faster pace and lower bounce of the balls – to deliver his best result yet. He defeated the big-serving American, Taylor Dent, ranked 30th in the world, on his way to the third round.

'Bottle this feeling, Andy, and then multiply it by ten when you're at Wimbledon,' Petch advised.

Two weeks later, when he walked through the iron gates of the All England Club, past the ivy-clad walls of Centre Court, through the corridors that oozed history and into the immaculate dressing room, Andy knew he was in a very special place.

'This feels different to any other tournament,' he said. 'So many legendary champions have walked down these same corridors and sat in this very dressing room.'

'You too could have your name engraved on that famous trophy one day,' said Petch before bringing

his player back to reality, 'but right now you need
to concentrate on your first-round match against
George Bastl.'

Andy rose to the challenge. Boosted by some
tremendous support, he eased past the Swiss player
for the loss of just eight games. Two days later, it
got even better as he knocked out the No. 14 seed
Radek Štepánek.

Andy had steamrolled into the third round without
even dropping a set.

'My first match was on Court No. 2, today I was
on Court No. 1. Do you think there's any chance I
could be on Centre Court next?' he asked Petch that
evening. Centre Court was the most famous court in
the whole of tennis.

'You never know, Andy. You're the last British
player left in the draw, so there's every chance. But
wherever you play, it will be really tough – you're
up against David Nalbandian, who reached the final
three years ago.'

Andy gulped.

Two days later, when his wish was granted and

he walked onto Centre Court, Andy banished any nerves. To the delight of the 15,000-strong crowd, and millions more watching on TV, he raced into a two-set lead against a stunned Nalbandian.

Andy had never played in an atmosphere like this before. The whole crowd seemed to be chanting his name, making the hairs on the back of his neck stand up.

'Come on, Andy.'

'Let's go, Andy, let's go. Let's go, Andy, let's go,' they cheered in between points, wildly waving their Union flags.

But Nalbandian hadn't got all the way to the Wimbledon final by fluke. He was one of the best grass-court players on the tour, and eventually the Argentine settled into the match and used all his experience to shut out the crowd and win the next two sets.

Never before in his career had Andy played in a match that had gone to five sets.

'This is exhausting,' he panted after another energy-sapping rally.

He gave everything he had but there was nothing left in the tank. An extremely relieved Nalbandian proved too strong in the final set, bringing Andy's Wimbledon dream to an end – until the next year at any rate.

'I was so close to a place in the fourth round,' a dejected Andy said afterwards.

'It's a sign of how far you've come that you're upset at not making the last sixteen of the biggest tournament in the world,' Petch replied. 'There'll be plenty more chances. I played here for more than ten years and you've already equalled my best Wimbledon performance at your first attempt.'

CHAPTER 8

A RIVALRY REBORN

Andy's heroic Wimbledon performances made the tennis world stand up and take notice. The experts were full of praise for the young Scot:

'He has a wonderful range of shots, the perfect mix of skill and strength.'

'A great tennis brain for a teenager. If he can continue to develop at such a rate, there's no reason he can't be a top ten player one day.'

'I haven't seen someone return the ball as well as that since Andre Agassi.'

That last sentence made Andy glow with pride. There was no higher honour than being compared to his tennis idol.

But while it was nice to hear such kind words, Andy knew full well that's all they were – *words*. If he was to make the most of his potential and become a top player, he would have to knuckle down and work harder than ever before in his life.

So that's exactly what he did.

His world ranking had risen almost a hundred places after Wimbledon and it continued to soar throughout the rest of 2005. Highlights included beating British No. 1 Tim Henman ('the greatest win of my career') and playing world No. 1 Roger Federer in his first ATP World Tour final. Andy might have lost the match, but the experience was invaluable.

'Well played, Andy. That was a tough match,' Roger said as he gave his opponent a warm handshake at the net. 'I lost my first final too, and it only made me more hungry to win the next one.'

When he checked the world rankings the following week, this time Andy didn't have to scroll down too far before finding his name.

'I've done it!' he cried out to Jamie. 'World number seventy-two.'

'Great work. You've achieved your goal of breaking into the top one hundred with three months to spare,' Jamie replied, patting his brother on the back. 'Do you think you'll be able to make it into the top ten by Christmas?'

'Don't be mad,' Andy grinned, although he was already setting his sights on some new goals.

A first ATP World Tour title was next on his list – and, just like Roger had said, he was absolutely ravenous to win one. He didn't have too much longer to wait, beating Australia's Lleyton Hewitt in the final of the SAP Open in February 2006. A couple of weeks later came the icing on the cake when he officially became the No. 1 ranked British player.

'I can't believe I'm now placed above Tim Henman and Greg Rusedski,' he said to his mother Judy. 'They've done so much for British tennis and I've learned loads from both of them since turning professional.'

The British public delighted in the performances of their new No. 1 at Wimbledon later that year, as Andy went one step better than in 2005, and reached the fourth round. His victory over third seed Andy Roddick encouraged the fans to dream that they could see another British champion at Wimbledon … at long last.

'When did a British man last win at Wimbledon?'

'Not in your lifetime. They didn't even have TV back then, it was so long ago.'

'Wasn't it Fred Perry?'

'Fred who?'

If Andy was to emulate the legendary Fred Perry, who won three Wimbledon titles in a row from 1934–6, it would not be with Petch, however.

In July 2006, he employed Brad Gilbert as his new coach. One of the most respected coaches on the circuit, Brad was in Roddick's corner when he won the US Open in 2004 and, most excitingly for Andy, had been by Andre Agassi's side for six of his Grand Slam titles.

'There's no doubt you're a terrifically talented player, Andy, and I want to help you get even better,' Brad explained.

'What do I need to focus on, Brad?' asked Andy, as hungry as ever to learn more.

'I want to focus on two key things: developing the tactical side of your game and improving your fitness and diet. If you want to compete with the very best players, particularly over the five-set matches at the Grand Slams, you need to be the fittest player on the court. And that means no more baguettes with chocolate spread or frappuccinos!'

'How did you even know…?' Andy's voice trailed off as he smiled sheepishly, recalling the coffees his mum would get for him from the local Starbucks during Wimbledon. At the same time, though, he was impressed by what his new coach was saying, as well as by his level of research.

With a new fitness regime in place, Andy continued to climb the world rankings. By October, as he prepared for the Madrid Masters, he was inside the world's top twenty. He was no longer daunted by any opponent, whatever their ranking, as he proved in the second round when knocking out third seed Ivan Ljubičić.

But his next opponent was different to all
the others – his old friend, and now foe, Novak
Djokovic.

The pair had seen each other many times since
their first meeting as juniors in France, practising
together and playing the occasional match, but this
was their first clash on the ATP World Tour. Their
careers had followed remarkably similar paths as they
rose up the rankings together, and Novak was seeded
No. 15 for this tournament, just above Andy.

'This is a bit different from the first match we ever
played in France, isn't it?' said Andy, gazing around
at the packed Madrid stadium.

'We were lucky to even get ball boys back then,'
Novak laughed.

Novak's laughter quickly stopped when the match
got underway, as Andy raced out of the blocks to
take the first set 6–1. But, like Andy, Novak was
made of much steelier stuff these days. He hit back
to edge the second set 7–5 before winning the
decider 6–3.

Andy was furious that he'd let such a good

opportunity slip away. It always hurt when he lost, and even more so when it was against his old practice partner. He didn't even hear Novak's words of commiseration as they shook hands.

Instead, he was already thinking about what he could do to beat his rival next time.

CHAPTER 9

BIRTHDAY BLUES

'What a way to spend my birthday,' Andy grumbled.

It should have been a special day as he celebrated leaving behind his teenage years and turning twenty, but instead he was speaking to his mum Judy from a hospital room in Hamburg.

'I got a birthday surprise all right – just not a very good one!'

A few hours earlier, Andy had been cruising to victory against the talented Italian Filippo Volandri in the first round of the Hamburg Masters. Leading 5–1, he went to play a routine forehand and...

'Aaarrrggghhh!'

Andy crumpled to the floor as he felt the most excruciating pain in his wrist. It was even worse than when he lost his fingernail all those years ago. He was forced to take an injury timeout to receive treatment from the physio, but insisted on carrying on and returning to the court.

He hit one more forehand…

'Aaaaaarrrrrrggggggghhhhhh!'

It was even worse than before. Andy hated withdrawing from any tournament but there was no way he could continue. As he packed his bag and headed to the hospital for a scan, there was only one thing he could think about.

'When will I be back?'

The injury could not have come at a worse time. Only a month earlier, he had broken into the world's top 10 for the first time, thanks to a strong performance in Miami. His run to the final had been ended by Novak Djokovic. He was itching for the chance to get revenge against his rival, but now he would be stuck twiddling his thumbs on the sidelines for weeks or, even worse, months.

Andy was a bag of nerves as he waited for the result of his scan.

'Please tell me I can play again, doc. I don't know what I'd do without tennis – and there's no way I'm going back to school.'

The doctor smiled.

'That has to be a good sign, right?' thought Andy as he ruffled his hands through his curly hair. 'Unless he takes pleasure in seeing other people suffer!'

'Andy, I'm pleased to report that you haven't broken anything in your wrist. You have injured the tendons, but there's no reason to believe that everything won't be back to normal when it's healed.'

'When will that be, doc?' Andy asked, not daring to look up from his seat.

'I would recommend a rest period of two to three months.'

Andy did a quick calculation in his head before letting out a pained groan, much to the surprise of the startled doctor who had assumed he'd delivered some relatively positive news.

His patient uttered just one more word before departing: 'Wimbledon…'

Andy realised that dealing with injuries was part of being a professional sportsperson, but that didn't make it any easier – he hated sitting around at home. His spell on the sidelines was even harder to stomach as he would be forced to miss his favourite tournament of the year.

In order to ease the frustration, he was planning to avoid all coverage and any mention of Wimbledon completely, but then he received a request he couldn't refuse.

'Why don't you come and watch me play?' suggested Jamie.

'Don't get me wrong,' said Andy. 'I love Wimbledon and of course I want to cheer you on, but I'm not sure I'd be very good at sitting still in the stands when all I want to do is to be out on court playing.'

'Come on, what else are you going to do? Play FIFA on the PlayStation for two weeks? It would mean a lot to me to have your support.'

'Okay then. Just don't get knocked out in the first round!'

In his brother's absence from the tournament, Jamie flew the flag for Britain with pride, teaming up with Jelena Janković from Serbia in the mixed doubles to advance all the way to the final.

The story captivated the British fans, who gave Jamie an ear-splitting reception for the final against Jonas Björkman and Alicia Molik. And there in the Centre Court crowd, living and breathing every point, was his biggest fan of all.

'Come on, Jamie!'

'Great volley!'

'Brilliant smash – I wonder who taught you that shot!'

Andy roared his support throughout the match and, when Jamie hit the winning volley on championship point, his brother leapt to his feet in delight.

Jamie had become the first Briton in twenty years to win a title at Wimbledon. As he watched his brother collect the trophy after the match, Andy could not have been any prouder. But at the same time, a little voice in his head kept saying over and over: 'I want a bit of that too.'

CHAPTER 10

THE FINAL HURDLE

'If Novak Djokovic can win a Grand Slam, then so can you.'

In the immediate aftermath of the 2008 Australian Open final, those words – from his new coach Miles Maclagan – made Andy feel a lot better.

His Serbian rival had just won his first Grand Slam title with victory over Jo-Wilfried Tsonga, the same player who had knocked Andy out of the tournament in the very first round.

While Andy was happy for his old sparring partner to have broken his Grand Slam duck, he would have loved to be standing there in his place.

Miles had taken over from Brad Gilbert as Andy's

coach at the end of 2007, a few months after he had returned to action from his wrist injury. While Brad had achieved a lot in a short space of time, Andy had often clashed with him.

Andy wasn't the type of person who would suffer in silence when he was unhappy or something was going wrong on court, and sometimes his temper might boil over – as any spectators sitting within earshot would testify.

'It's okay to be angry, Andy, but we need to use that passion to bring out your best performances,' said Miles. 'There are times when it's good to be aggressive, but it's also important to stay cool in the heat of the moment. That could be vital in your bid to win a Grand Slam.'

Andy's ears perked up. 'Win a Grand Slam.' He was now a regular winner on the tour and firmly entrenched in the top 10 – and the next step in his career was to win a Grand Slam tournament. Just like Novak had done…

Andy was getting a bit fed up at the thought of Novak, let alone actually playing him. Not that he'd admit it to anybody, of course. The two players who were born just a week apart had taken very similar journeys to tennis stardom, but Andy realised the Serbian held the upper hand at the moment. He had won all three of their ATP World Tour matches so far and, a few months after his Australian Open triumph, he made it four in a row.

'The result had better be different next time…' Andy barked at Miles as he stormed off the court in Monte Carlo '…or else you'll see me get *really* angry!'

He had to wait two more months for his next opportunity in Canada. This time, there were no more outbursts – much to the relief of Miles and the rest of the coaching team – as he finally stopped the rot. Novak had no answer as Andy used his aggression to maximum effect to win in straight sets.

That performance gave him extra confidence for the pair's next meeting the following month in Cincinnati. The stakes were even higher this time – Andy was gunning for the biggest result of his career, his first Masters title.

With both players so keen for victory, there was very little to choose between them. Andy just edged the first set, taking it in a tiebreak, but he knew the job was only half-done.

'Keep cool, just like Miles said,' he told himself in between bites of a banana during the break after the first set.

Nerves, however, played a big part as the match progressed, with both players producing moments of magic as well as some basic errors. It was Andy who handled the situation better, though, with some inspired rallying taking him to within one point of the title.

'Just one more point...'

But Novak wasn't prepared to give up yet. He saved the first match point. And the second one. And then the third. By the time Andy had squandered five match points, he was starting to despair.

'Is there any way past this guy? It feels like there are five Novaks out there!'

As the second set went to another tiebreak, the odds were stacked in the Serbian's favour. But although he was dejected, Andy was learning how to control his emotions. He knew that he could experience good times and bad times on the court, and it was how he dealt with those moments that affected the outcome of the match. Instead of thinking about the match points that slipped away, he focused on the positives.

'You've already beaten him once this year. There's no reason why you can't do it again.'

'Remember what happened in the first-set tiebreak? You won. Go out there and do it again.'

The tiebreak was a nail-biter. With the scores level at 4–4, the players served up a spectacular point that will live long in the memory of anyone lucky enough to be in the crowd. An unforgettable twenty-five-stroke rally unfolded, with Andy's blistering power blocked out by Novak's ironman defence, before he finally won it with a stunning cross-court backhand.

Both players gasped for air at the end of the rally, and this time – at last – Novak had nothing left.

Two points later, Andy was the champion. He sunk

to his knees and thumped the ball into the jubilant crowd.

Looking more like two exhausted boxers who had just slugged out twelve rounds in the ring, the players hugged at the net – a sign of the respect they shared for each other.

'Well done, Andy. That was one of my hardest matches. You are a truly deserving champion.'

'Thanks Novak. Perhaps next time you could let me win a little more easily!'

With back-to-back victories under his belt, Andy's confidence was sky high ahead of the final Grand Slam event of the season. After two routine wins in the US Open in September 2008, he found himself two sets down to Austria's Jürgen Melzer. But Andy didn't know when he was beaten – he showed the benefits of his intense training regime to fight back and win in five sets.

He faced an even tougher challenge in the semi-finals against Rafael Nadal, the world No. 1 and all-round superstar from Spain, who had won all five of their previous matches. That run had included a victory in the quarter-finals at Wimbledon a few months earlier which ended Andy's dream there for another year.

But now it was time for Andy to finally raise his game against Rafa, eventually closing out a match that was played over two days due to rain delays.

'I knew all those hours we played in the rain in Dunblane would come in handy one day,' he joked with Judy afterwards.

There was no laughter, however, on the morning of the 2008 US Open final as Andy thought about the mammoth task that lay ahead. He was the first British player to reach a Grand Slam final since Greg Rusedski eleven years earlier, and was bidding to become the first British man to win one since 1936. And if he was to wipe out seventy-two years of suffering for the British public, he would have to overcome the sizeable obstacle in his way called Roger Federer.

Andy was bubbling with confidence, but playing against the standout player of the decade put some doubts in his mind.

'He's practically unbeatable here. He's won the last four US Opens,' Andy said to Miles with a furrowed brow.

'You've had a year of firsts, Andy – beating Novak, beating Rafa, your first Masters title. Who's to say you can't have another one with a first Grand Slam success?'

The answer came in New York a few hours later. Try as he might, Andy just couldn't replicate the form that had served him so well in the previous rounds. He lost in three sets, as Roger triumphed yet again.

To stand any chance against Roger, Andy knew he had to be at the very top of his game, and that hadn't happened. He also knew, having played in one Grand Slam final, that he was desperate to be in another one. Very soon.

CHAPTER 11

FRIENDS REUNITED

'I don't know why they call them "Grand". Grand old waste of time is all they are.'

Andy was fed up, but he realised if he carried on grumbling much longer, his girlfriend Kim would become fed up of listening to him.

The problem was a familiar one: despite a couple more near misses, he was still no nearer to getting his hands on a Grand Slam trophy.

His latest disappointment had come in the 2011 Australian Open final where he was outfoxed by Novak Djokovic. Exactly a year earlier, he had suffered the same fate, at the same stage, against Roger Federer.

'It's just my luck to have been born at the same time as three of the greatest players in history,' he complained.

Since Roger's breakthrough win at Wimbledon back in 2003, the Swiss maestro and Rafa Nadal had won twenty-five Grand Slams between them. Now Novak was getting in on the act too; Andy's old rival was on his way to recording one of the greatest individual seasons in tennis history, where he would lose just six matches. And it was hard to watch.

'Can't they let someone else have a turn?'

At times like this, Kim was the perfect sounding board for Andy. A passionate supporter in the stands, away from the court she was a calming, reassuring influence and happy to listen to his concerns.

'Just think how much better you've become *because* you've been up against those players,' Kim said. 'They've made you raise your game to a level you could never have imagined.'

Andy nodded. He knew Kim was right – again. Kim's father Nigel was a top tennis coach and he had passed on all his knowledge to his daughter. She had a knack for knowing when to hand out advice and when to keep her thoughts to herself, which Andy really appreciated. His career had flourished ever since they started going out together back in 2005.

Kim wasn't the only familiar face in the stands these days. After splitting from his coach Miles Maclagan in 2010, Andy decided to ask an old friend to help out while he planned his next move.

'What took you so long to call? Did you lose my number?' said the voice at the other end of the line.

'Er, well, I'm sorry, Dani. I've been really busy, you see, what with all the tournaments this year and, um, travelling… and then I was injured…'

He was interrupted by fits of laughter.

'Don't be crazy, man! I'm kidding – and you still fall for it, just like you always did back in Barcelona. It's great to hear from you.'

Andy grinned. After all these years, he should have known Dani Vallverdu was pulling his leg. Their tennis careers had followed different paths since their days as teenagers in Barcelona. Dani had gone on to represent Venezuela in the Davis Cup but never quite made it as a player at the top level, and had now turned his attention to coaching. They had managed to keep in touch over the years – and Dani never failed to put a smile on Andy's face.

After ten minutes of chatting, catching up on all their news and some more teasing, Andy finally cut to the chase.

'So, Dani, I'd like you to be part of my coaching team. Your main role will be on the other side of the net as my hitting partner. Do you fancy it?'

'It sounds great,' his friend replied. 'Just don't get upset when I keep beating you!'

The move was a masterstroke. As well as having a partner on the court he loved practising with, Andy now had a partner in crime off the court. At times, Andy found that being a professional tennis player was a lonely existence, travelling from country to country, and hotel room to hotel room, but that wasn't a problem with Dani around. He was always happy to watch football, talk boxing, pull pranks, play games, have a go on the PlayStation

– essentially do whatever Andy needed to take his mind off the tennis.

'This is the best job in the world,' Dani said one day.

'It will be even better when you help me win my first Grand Slam,' Andy replied.

As the 2011 season drew to a close, Andy was confident that his moment would finally arrive the following year. Crucially, everything was going well behind the scenes. His family played a big part in his success – Kim and Judy now attended any tournaments they could, while he would often see Jamie when they played at the same events. With Dani on board, he had an outstanding support team.

There was just one piece of the puzzle left to fill.

CHAPTER 12

KEEP BELIEVING

'Happy New Year!'

Andy was in the mood to celebrate.

As the clock struck midnight, he could finally wave goodbye to 2011 and its memories of Grand Slam misery, and look forward to what promised to be the biggest year of his life.

He was playing as well as ever, and had high hopes of winning a precious Grand Slam trophy. What's more, 2012 would be an extra special year for every British sportsperson – the Olympic Games were taking place in London that summer.

Andy loved the Olympics almost as much as he adored tennis, and the Olympic tennis tournament would take place just a short drive from his home.

There was one more reason to celebrate that evening. A few hours earlier, Andy had announced that Ivan Lendl would be his new coach. Behind every good player there is a good coach, and Andy had worked with some of the best tennis brains over the years. This time, though, there was a key difference, as he explained to Jamie.

'When he was a player, Ivan won eight Grand Slam titles. If anyone can teach me what I need to do to win the biggest tournaments, it's him.'

'I hear he's the ironman of tennis and doesn't take any nonsense, so make sure you listen to him more carefully than you did at school,' Jamie joked.

Even when Andy lost again to Novak at the Australian Open in January, having come within a whisker of winning their titanic semi-final, the result didn't puncture his positive mood for long. He was working harder than ever before and knew if he kept playing the same way, and putting in the same effort, the rewards would come. Maybe, just maybe, at Wimbledon that summer.

If Andy could win the Wimbledon title, he would

achieve something his coach had never managed. Despite all his success, that particular trophy had always eluded Ivan, much to his dismay.

'Grass is for cows, not tennis players,' he said to Andy, echoing the same comments he had made in his playing days. 'I have bad memories of Wimbledon but if you can win here, it will make me very happy.'

'Me too,' thought Andy. 'As well as sixty-odd million Brits!'

For two glorious weeks, Andy gave the country a tournament to remember. He started in style, losing only six games to Nikolay Davydenko. Ivo Karlović, the man who boasted the fastest serve in the game, was then swatted aside, with Andy making his service look about as deadly as an adoring puppy.

In the third round, Marcos Baghdatis was Andy's next victim, in a match that didn't finish until after 11p.m. under the Centre Court roof.

'Next time can you wrap it up a bit earlier please?' joked Dani. 'It's way past my bedtime.'

'Sorry, I know you need all the beauty sleep you can get!' Andy shot back quick as a flash.

Andy next defeated Marin Čilić and David Ferrer before overpowering Jo-Wilfried Tsonga in the semi-final. Six of the toughest opponents had tried to derail Andy's Wimbledon bid, to no avail, but an even harder challenge awaited him in the decider.

'Not Roger again,' groaned Andy on the morning of the final.

Dani tried to boost his friend's confidence. 'Your previous Grand Slam finals have been on hard courts. This one is on grass, so it's bound to be different.'

'I agree,' Andy replied glumly. 'Different as in even tougher. Do you know he's won six times already here?'

For once, Dani was lost for words.

It was left to Ivan to pick up Andy's spirits.

'I don't care if Roger has won here six times or sixty times. That is in the past. It's 2012 and you are the best player at this tournament right now.'

Andy beamed. Over the past six months, Ivan had focused his mind on thinking positively – and right now he felt like he could beat anyone.

That afternoon, Andy marched onto Centre Court looking like a man who belonged there. Oozing confidence, he flew out of the blocks to win the first set against the stunned Swiss player. The crowd went berserk.

'You can do it, Andy.'

'Two more sets to make history.'

'We love you, Andy.'

The feeling was mutual. Andy loved playing in front of his home crowd. While there was enormous pressure on him to deliver, it also brought the best out of him. He wanted nothing more than to give the fans the win they craved so badly.

Roger loved the Wimbledon crowd, too. After the shock of the first set, the old master raised his game to another level to square the match.

'You'll get your Wimbledon win one day, my British friend,' he said to himself. 'Just not this year, I'm afraid.'

With a record-equalling seventh victory firmly in his sights, he would not be denied. The next two sets were closely fought, but both went Roger's way and, before long, he was hoisting the famous gold cup in the air yet again.

Andy had come so close to achieving his dream, only for it to be snatched away. In his interview after the match with the BBC's Sue Barker, it was all too much for him. He choked on his words, then broke down in tears.

Later, when he had finally said farewell to the fans and retreated to the dressing room, he felt embarrassed. 'I can't believe I cried on national TV. I'll never live it down.'

Kim put a gentle arm around her boyfriend. 'You should be proud of yourself. Those tears showed the public just how much you care. They'll love you even more now.'

'They won't love me if I keep losing Grand Slams. That's four losing finals in a row,' Andy said as Ivan joined them in the dressing room.

'I lost my first four Grand Slam finals too,' Ivan revealed. 'And do you know what happened the fifth time?'

'What?'

'I won,' before adding with a chuckle, 'but at no point did I ever cry!'

CHAPTER 13

OLYMPIC DREAM

'Here we go again.'

Three weeks after losing the biggest match of his life, Andy was back at Wimbledon.

'I must be a glutton for punishment,' he joked with Jamie as they walked through the iron gates and headed towards the dressing room.

'It will be different this time – you've got me on your side!'

Jamie was right. It *was* different. The dust had barely settled on that year's Grand Slam event, and now Wimbledon was open for business again, hosting the London 2012 Olympic tennis tournament.

Except it wasn't the Wimbledon that Andy knew. Of course, Centre Court was in the same place and the grass was as green as ever, but other things jumped out at him. Music was booming around the grounds and everywhere he looked he spotted the famous Olympic rings.

Suddenly, an almighty roar rose from one of the outside courts in the distance.

Andy looked at Jamie with an excited grin. 'The fans always give good support here, but I've never heard a noise *that* loud.'

'It will be even louder when we get out there.'

The brothers were representing Great Britain in the first round of the men's doubles. And that meant, instead of the traditional white clothing that players normally had to wear at Wimbledon, they would be dressed in the red, white and blue of Team GB.

Andy always jumped at the chance to represent his country and couldn't wait to get out there and give the fans something to cheer about.

Unfortunately, their Austrian opponents, Jürgen Melzer and Alexander Peya, hadn't read the script and played the role of party poopers to perfection, beating the brothers in straight sets.

'Here we go again,' Andy muttered as he trudged off court.

'At least you've got two more chances in the singles and mixed doubles. That's the end of my Olympics. Make sure you take your opportunity and bring home a gold for Team GB,' a disappointed Jamie urged his brother.

The next day, Andy set about his task with relish. Resuming the fine run of form he had shown only a few weeks earlier, he breezed past his first four opponents to reach the semi-finals.

The incredible atmosphere brought the best out of him. In between points, fans waved flags and chanted songs.

There's only one Andy Murray
One Andy Murray
Walking along
Singing a song
Walking in a Murray wonderland

'It feels like I'm in a football stadium,' Andy thought as he gazed around Centre Court at the fans standing arm-in-arm. 'I don't ever want this tournament to end.'

In the semi-finals, Andy faced an opponent who had grown accustomed to ending his tournaments.

'Not this time, Novak,' Andy murmured under his breath as the pair stared at each other across the net before the start of the match. 'Not at my home Olympics, in front of these amazing fans.'

He was true to his word, resisting an almighty challenge from the player who had won the Wimbledon title a year earlier, and winning 7–5, 7–5.

'Well played, Andy. Now go out there and win gold for your country,' said Novak to his old friend. While they were fierce rivals on the court, they always showed each other respect at the end of each match.

Andy was now guaranteed to win a silver medal, but all he could think about was gold. Team GB was enjoying an unforgettable Games, winning a sackful of medals, and Andy wanted to join the gold rush.

In order to do so, he would have to succeed where he had failed a few weeks earlier. Roger Federer was waiting for him in the final.

'This is your time, Andy,' Ivan advised his player that evening. He wasn't attending the matches but he called Andy every day to give him some tips. 'Keep banging on the door, and eventually it will burst open.'

While Andy was sad Ivan couldn't be at the Olympics in person, he was relieved that there was a perfectly good substitute taking his place – someone he knew all too well.

'Don't think you're getting an easy time because Ivan's not here,' Dani laughed as he had a final practice hit with Andy before the final. As coach of the British Olympic tennis team, Dani had been by Andy's side throughout the tournament – and his presence helped him relax before the massive test that lay ahead.

An Olympic singles gold medal was practically

the only prize in tennis that Roger had not won. To make matters even harder, unlike the previous rounds, the final was a best-of-five sets match, so Andy would have to win three sets against the world's greatest player.

But he wasn't bothered. With the patriotic British crowd on his side, he would have happily played all day and night. The first set came and went in a flash, with Andy taking it 6–2. In the Wimbledon final, Roger had lost the first set and then rebounded to win, but Andy wasn't letting any negative thoughts enter his head.

'This time it's different,' he told himself.

It got even better in the second set, which Andy wrapped up 6–1. He was in complete control, at one point winning nine games in a row. The crowd was in full voice.

'Let's go, Andy, let's go.'

'GB, GB, GB.'

'This is the most fun I've ever had at a tournament,' Andy thought as the spectators jumped up to do a Mexican wave around Centre Court. In fact, he was having such a good time, and playing so well, that he almost forgot he was on the brink of history.

Ever the fighter, Roger refused to throw in the towel in the third set but he could not contend with his opponent's pile-driving shots and frightening accuracy. With less than two hours on the clock, Andy brought up match point before finishing the job in suitably speedy style – with an ace.

Andy put his head in his hands. He could barely believe what he had just done.

He was the new Olympic champion.

As the fans roared their appreciation, Andy climbed up to the box where his family were sitting with his coaching team. He was quickly swallowed up in a sea of hugs.

'You're my hero,' shouted Kim.

'You have worked so hard for this,' Judy added. 'You deserve this gold medal more than anyone.'

'It's not just for me, Mum. This is a gold medal for all of Great Britain.'

Later that afternoon, a somewhat exhausted Andy

was back on court to win a silver medal alongside Laura Robson in the final of the mixed doubles event. Of all the incredible performances by British athletes at the Olympics, Andy's achievements were up there with the very best.

He left Wimbledon that evening with a gold and silver medal around his neck. Not bad for an afternoon's work.

CHAPTER 14

THE WAIT IS OVER

"GOLDEN BOY"

"MURRAY MANIA"

"BRITAIN'S GOT TALENT... AND ANOTHER GOLD"

Andy chuckled at the headlines as he munched his cornflakes. It was the morning after his Olympic triumph, and his face was plastered all over the newspapers – front page and back page.

It was nice to see that the country was getting so excited at his success, but he had never allowed himself to get too carried away with what the media said or wrote about him – good or bad.

That wasn't about to change now.

'Right,' he said to Kim as he got up from the breakfast table. 'That's enough of that. It's time to focus on my next challenge. Do you know there are only thirty-five days to go?'

'Thirty-five days?' Kim asked with a raised eyebrow. It had been such a whirlwind summer she was struggling to remember what month it was, let alone looking five weeks ahead.

'That's how many days there are until the US Open final,' he said, picking up his tennis bag. 'And there's no way I'm going to miss that.'

'Don't you ever get tired?' Kim asked but there was no answer, only the sound of the front door closing. Andy was heading off to practice again, less than twenty-four hours after winning Olympic gold.

Kim was happy to let him go. She had nothing but admiration for her boyfriend's dedication to his career. Andy had always been a hard worker, but there was now an aura of confidence around him that she had never sensed before.

Later that day, as Andy powered forehands,

backhands and volleys to every corner of the court, Dani noticed that confidence too.

'Hey, go easy on me, man! It's like there are three Andys out here today – and I struggle to keep up with just one of you.'

Andy took that confidence with him all the way across the Atlantic to New York:

'When I won the Junior US Open here eight years ago, I dreamed of coming back one day to win the senior title. I feel like that time has come.'

'Okay,' said his coach Ivan, 'but remember there are seven very talented opponents standing in your way, and they will all be desperate to beat the new Olympic champion.'

Andy nodded. Just like when he read the papers, he wasn't about to get carried away.

Seeded No. 3 for the US Open, he lived up to his star billing by breezing through the early rounds with the minimum of fuss to reach the quarter-finals.

'This is where the tournament starts to get tough,' he said to Ivan before his match against Marin Čilić.

He made it even tougher for himself by dropping

the first set to the Croatian, but then showed the steely resolve that had become such a strong part of his game to win the next three sets.

Semi-final – same story. This time it was Tomáš Berdych who nabbed the opening set before Andy turned the match around. He raced through the next three sets to seal his spot in the final.

'Well done, son,' Judy said afterwards, 'but it would help my nerves if you started your matches a little better!'

Andy knew he wouldn't be able to start slowly in his next match. Novak Djokovic would never let him get away with that in the final.

As defending champion and the winner of their only previous Grand Slam final, Novak was the favourite, but Andy quietly fancied his chances of setting the record straight. He thought back to the Olympics. 'Remember what happened last time you played.'

Kim, Judy, Ivan and Dani were all in the massive 23,000-strong crowd that flocked into the Arthur Ashe Stadium for the final. The two players quickly set about giving the spectators a match to remember.

In a draining first set, they threw everything at each other, shot for shot, smash for smash. With the scores level at 6–6, they needed a tiebreak to decide the winner, but even that wasn't simple. Eventually, after twenty-four minutes and six set points, Andy was victorious. It was the longest tiebreak in the tournament's history.

'I've played entire matches that have been shorter than that set,' Andy thought as he took a well-earned rest in between sets.

The see-sawing second set also went Andy's way. He was on the verge of making history. It had been 76 years, and 237 Grand Slam events, since a British man had last won one of the four major tournaments. Now Andy was just one set away from ending the drought.

Judy and Kim cheered wildly in the stands. Even Ivan – who rarely showed any emotion behind his sunglasses – was looking excited.

'Keep your cool. This is not over yet,' Andy told himself.

Having played against Novak for so many years,

he knew his old enemy would never give in, and so it proved as the reigning champion roared back into contention. He claimed the third set 6–2 before closing out the fourth 6–3.

Andy was shell-shocked. The match was suddenly level again. He looked up at the stands to see the worried faces of Judy and Kim staring back at him.

Something had to change.

He had to stop Novak's momentum.

And so he went for a loo break.

With the noise from the screaming fans fading as he left the court, Andy finally had time to gather his thoughts. He stared at himself in the mirror. He thought of all the support and encouragement he had received from family, friends and fans, and all the words of advice from Ivan, his coaching team and fitness trainers.

But they could only help him get so far. Andy knew that if he was going to win a Grand Slam, it was ultimately up to him and no one else.

'Get back out there and for one set give it everything you've got,' he said to himself. 'Don't come off that court with any regrets.'

It was a surprised Novak who looked up to see his sprightly opponent bounce back on to court for the start of the fifth set.

Was this the same player who had limped off a few minutes earlier?

Andy was a new man. They might have been playing for more than four hours, but he felt like it was the first rally of the match as he chased the ball all over the court like a greyhound hunting down a hare. He raced into a 3–0 lead. He was in no mood to lose his advantage again.

A few games later, he had match point.

Novak hit a forehand. It went high and long.

'Keep going. Keep going. Keep…'

'Out!'

He had done it.

'Game, set and match, Murray.'

Novak was beaten.

'Murray wins 7–6, 7–5, 2–6, 3–6, 6–2.'

Andy had won a Grand Slam.

In the dressing room, long after he had collected his trophy and all the fans had gone home, Andy was almost too tired and too sore to celebrate. The match had lasted six minutes shy of five hours, and when he took one of his socks off, he realised he had run so hard that he'd lost two toenails.

'That reminds me of the time you lost your fingernail when your brother...'

'Not now, Mum,' Andy interrupted Judy. 'No one wants to hear that story again!'

'I told you it would be fifth time lucky, Andy,' Ivan said, slapping the player on his back. 'Who cares about losing those four finals now?'

Andy beamed at his coach. 'I've forgotten them already, but I'll never forget this day as long as I live.'

CHAPTER 15

DARE TO DREAM

'It's not just cows that enjoy grass, Ivan. I love it too.'

Ivan smiled as he remembered the comment he had made to Andy a year earlier.

'I'm glad to hear it, but please don't think about giving up tennis to become a gardener just yet. This could be the best chance you'll ever get to win Wimbledon.'

It was the night before the 2013 championships, and Andy had enjoyed the perfect warm-up to the biggest tournament on the tennis calendar. Six miles up the road in London, just over the River Thames, he had won the Queen's Club title for the third time. That run of results took his record on grass surfaces to eleven wins in a row if you counted his Olympics achievement from a year earlier.

'It's funny. In the early years of my career, I used to think grass wasn't my best surface, as I had grown up playing on hard courts and on clay in Barcelona,' Andy said. 'But each year I have learned more about how to play on it, and got used to how the ball bounces, and now I feel like I'm a match for anyone – even Roger Federer.'

'You're absolutely right,' Ivan replied. 'Did you know that every time you have played at Wimbledon, you have always matched your effort from the previous year, or done even better?'

Not for the first time, Andy was impressed by his coach's knowledge. At times it seemed to him that Ivan had a book of stats inside his brain. He knew so much about the sport.

'And if you go one better than last year's final,' Ivan continued, 'you know what that means...'

'Steady on, coach. I haven't even played the first round yet.'

From the very first day, it became clear that the 2013 Wimbledon was going to be different. In one of the biggest shocks in the tournament's history, two-time champion Rafa Nadal crashed out in the first round. Then, on a day that became known as 'Wacky Wednesday', the defending champion Roger Federer also departed the tournament, together with many other highly-ranked seeds that performed disappointingly.

Andy, on the other hand, had no such problems. He eased through the first four rounds without losing a set, in the process passing Fred Perry's British record for the most Grand Slam matches won.

'I'm sure I'll look back on this record with pride when I've finished my playing career, but right now there's only one record of Fred's I'm interested in matching – and that's winning Wimbledon,' he said to Judy after knocking out Russia's Mikhail Youzhny in the fourth round.

It had been seventy-seven long years since Fred had won the title. With Rafa and Roger out of contention, and with Andy in top form, the fans excitedly waited to see if another British man might finally be crowned champion

However, Andy was well aware that his performances in the early rounds didn't count for anything.

'It's good to get through the first week without playing any long matches, so I'm fresh for what comes next, but no one wins the trophy in the quarter-finals,' he told his mum. 'They only lose it.'

Those words very nearly came back to haunt him two days later. Trailing by two sets to Spain's Fernando Verdasco in their quarter-final, Andy stood on the brink of defeat. He hadn't been playing badly in those early sets; the problem was his opponent had been playing as if he was from another planet.

But Andy was not prepared to give up, and nor were the fans who continued to shout their support.

'Keep on fighting and your chance will come. You can't let this amazing crowd down,' Andy thought, although he was actually struggling to hear himself think above the deafening noise from the spectators.

Inspired by the fans and using all his grass-court

experience, he fought back. This was where all
the hard months of winter fitness training proved
worthwhile as he outran and outmuscled Verdasco.

Finally, Andy won in five sets, and had reached the
semi-finals by the skin of his teeth.

'That was so tough,' Andy said to Ivan afterwards.
'But no one hands out Grand Slam titles on a plate to
you. You have to earn them.'

'We both know that only too well,' Ivan replied.

Winning a Grand Slam semi-final is always a
tall order, and that was certainly the case for Andy
against Jerzy Janowicz – all 6ft 8in of him. At first,
Andy struggled to cope with his Polish opponent's
booming serve, and he lost the first set.

However, Andy refused to panic and slowly gained
the upper hand. By the start of the fourth set, he
was in control, having won five games in a row and
needing just one more set to reach the final.

But at that moment, the tournament referee
decided it was time to close the Centre Court roof
due to bad light. Play was stopped for half an hour.

Andy was furious at the disruption.

'What do you mean it's too dark?' he yelled at the referee. 'It's an outdoor tournament, it's not raining and it's the middle of summer!'

But it was no use. He had no choice.

Luckily, there was a calming presence waiting for him in the dressing room.

'Don't let it bother you, Andy,' Ivan said. 'You're in control of this match and one set away from a Wimbledon final. That's all that matters.'

Andy quickly regained his composure and, by the time he returned to the court, it was as if the episode had never happened. He finished the job with the loss of only three more games.

Twelve months after reaching his first Wimbledon final, he would contest the decider again. But this time it felt different. So much had changed since losing the final to Roger Federer the previous year. He had won Olympic gold on the same court. He had won his first Grand Slam title.

Andy was ready to make history.

CHAPTER 16

A DREAM COME TRUE

Andy gazed around Centre Court.

There was Manchester United striker Wayne Rooney. Hollywood film stars Bradley Cooper and Gerard Butler sat side by side, both dressed in exactly the same blue suit. Also present was former Spice Girl Victoria Beckham, who designed the dress Kim was wearing specially for the occasion. And then Andy saw the Prime Minister, David Cameron. He took a deep breath.

'Two minutes.'

The umpire's voice snapped him back to reality. In two minutes' time, he would be playing the biggest match of his life, on Wimbledon's Centre

Court, in front of some of the most famous faces on the planet. But he had no time to worry about them now. He had to focus on a racket, a small green ball and on defeating the man standing on the other side of the net.

'First set. Mr Djokovic to serve.'

It was no surprise to Andy that Novak was his opponent yet again. This was now their fourth meeting in a Grand Slam final after the Serbian had won the Australian Open earlier in the year. But they had never met in a Wimbledon final before, and Andy had an enormous advantage – the support of the crowd.

Of the 15,000 fans in the stands, Andy guessed that at least 14,900 of them were cheering for him. And that didn't include the thousands upon thousands of supporters crammed onto the hill behind Centre Court to watch the match on a big screen. There wasn't a single spare blade of grass to be found.

'I cannot believe all these people are here to watch me,' Andy thought. 'Let's give them something to shout about.'

When Andy broke Novak's serve to take an early lead, they went mad.

> *We love you, Andy, we do*
> *We love you, Andy, we do*
> *We love you, Andy, we do*
> *Oh, Andy, we love you!*

When Novak broke back to level the set, there was a collective groan and then a generous round of applause. While the fans were desperate for a British victory, they also had huge respect for Novak.

And when Andy hit back to win the first set, they exploded into song again.

> *Let's go, Andy, let's go*
> *Let's go, Andy, let's go.*

'Two more sets to go,' Andy said to himself as he took a long drink of water. It was a baking hot afternoon and it was important to have plenty of fluids. He knew he would need every last drop of his energy to beat Novak.

In the second set, Novak raced into a 4–1 lead. But helped by the raucous support of the crowd, and now wearing a cap to block out the sun, Andy pulled himself back into contention. Each time he won a crucial point, the fans roared.

It was the sweetest sound Andy had ever heard.

He was playing out of his skin and at 6–5 in the second set he held three points to seal a 2–0 lead. He only needed one of them.

Ace.

As the fans leapt to their feet again, Andy coolly pumped his fist and stared at Kim with a steely glare of determination.

'One more set to go.'

The carnival atmosphere continued in the third set. Andy took a 2–0 lead. Novak levelled it up at 2–2 before upping his game to lead 4–2. Andy in turn bounced back to 4–4.

'Talk about a roller coaster of emotions,' Kim said, shaking her head, before once again shouting the three words that rang around Centre Court all that afternoon.

'Come on, Andy!'

The topsy-turvy nature of the match continued in the next game as Andy dismantled Novak's serve to open up a 5–4 lead.

'One more game to go,' he told himself.

That was all he needed – one more game to become Wimbledon champion. Four more points.

After seventy-seven years of waiting, Andy wanted to get the job done as quickly as possible. He raced through the first three points to lead 40–0.

Cue pandemonium in the crowd. He had never heard such a noise in his life. It felt like the famous Centre Court was shaking.

As the umpire made the players wait until the noise died down, suddenly the significance of the moment hit him. If he won the next point, he was the Wimbledon champion. The prize he had dreamed of winning ever since he first hit a tennis ball.

'Just one more point…'

But he knew Novak wouldn't just let him win. In the

blink of an eye, the three match points came and went. All of a sudden, Novak had a point to win the game. Andy snuffed that out with a booming serve. Twice more, though, Novak held game point, once thanks to a shot that hit the top of the net, then trickled over.

It was one of the most exciting and nerve-wracking games in the history of tennis, and it just so happened that it was taking place in the Wimbledon final.

As the crowd lived, breathed, ooahed and aahed every point of every rally, Andy kept his cool to deny his opponent. Eventually, he held match point again.

'Let's finish the job.'

And this time, he did – with a big serve, and an even bigger forehand. As Novak's backhand hit the net, Andy dropped his racket in amazement. He threw his cap off, raised his hands in the air and screamed just one word.

'Yesssssssssssssss!'

He was so overcome with emotion that it was a few moments before he remembered to shake Novak's hand.

'Andy, you deserved to win today. Congratulations.'

'Thanks so much, Novak. That means a lot.'

It was time to celebrate. Andy charged into the crowd and climbed up to the box where Kim, Ivan, Dani and all the team were waiting to hug him.

'Well done, Andy.'

'You're a superstar.'

'What a match.'

Andy thanked each and every one of them. He knew how important a part they had played in his victory.

As he began to return to the court for the trophy ceremony, he heard a very familiar voice.

'Andy, over here!'

He looked up to see Judy waving wildly. In the madness of all the kisses and back-slapping, Andy had forgotten to thank his mum.

He rushed over and gave Judy a big hug.

'Sorry Mum.'

'Don't worry, Andy. I'll let you off just this once!'

CHAPTER 17

THE PEOPLE'S CHAMPION

The days that followed the Wimbledon win were a whirlwind for Andy. There were radio interviews, photoshoots, newspaper interviews, events with fans, TV interviews, trophy parades – and then some more interviews.

'And I thought playing tennis was tiring,' Andy said to Kim as he collapsed into a chair one evening. 'I need a rest.'

As exhausting as it was, he wouldn't have swapped it for anything. Winning Wimbledon was the culmination of a lifelong dream, and he was only too happy to share his joy with all the fans who had supported him along the way.

Unfortunately, the tennis calendar didn't allow much time for rest and, before he knew it, he was back on court, playing for Great Britain against Croatia in the Davis Cup. But it felt like a different Andy from the one who had wowed the Wimbledon crowd only weeks earlier.

Andy's back had been troubling him for some time and, after his team won, he decided enough was enough.

'I can't keep playing with my back like this,' he told Ivan. 'I need to get it fixed once and for all.'

'You know you could be out for several months if you have surgery.'

'If that's what it takes to ensure I can play for many more years, then I'm prepared to do it.'

While it was a disappointing way to end such a memorable year, Andy still had one big event to look forward to. He had been nominated for the 2013 BBC Sports Personality of the Year award, and the rumours were that he had a very strong chance of winning.

Not that he believed them.

'I've got no chance,' he said to Kim when he learned of his nomination. 'There are so many great sportsmen and women out there who deserve to win – Tony McCoy, Mo Farah, Christine Ohuruogu, Chris Froome...'

Kim cut him off. 'I agree, but none of them won *Wimbledon*, Andy. That tournament is so special to so many people.'

Unlike when he won the Young Sports Personality of the Year award nearly ten years earlier, there was no chance of Andy missing this ceremony due to any toilet troubles. In fact, he wasn't present for any of it as he was in Miami, recovering from back surgery and training for 2014.

Andy went to Miami every winter. It was a key part of his preparation for the new season and, while he was sad not to be at the ceremony, he knew it was the right decision to put his tennis career first. Besides, he had always loved Miami ever since his first visit with his mum and gran when he won the Junior Orange Bowl.

The British fans still got their chance to see Andy

as he joined the TV show via video link – it might have been winter back home, but Andy was standing in front of a swimming pool in the Florida sun.

He waited nervously as cyclist Bradley Wiggins, who had won in 2012, announced the winner.

'The 2013 Sports Personality of the Year is... Andy Murray.'

Andy couldn't believe it. Never did he think for one moment that his name would be read out. So many greats of British sport had won this special award – Chris Hoy, David Beckham, Paula Radcliffe, Steve Redgrave, to name only a few – and now he had joined that list. He felt extremely humbled as he collected the trophy from tennis legend Martina Navratilova.

'I'd like to thank all the public who voted, for giving me so much support over the last couple of years. It's made a huge difference,' Andy said.

Next, he had a special message for his family and support team.

'I couldn't have done it without you.'

There was another huge surprise that evening when Kim called to congratulate him.

'You received 401,470 votes, over 330,000 more than the runner-up, Welsh rugby player Leigh Halfpenny.'

Andy couldn't get his head around the sheer number of people who had taken the time to vote for him. 'I don't know 400 people, let alone 400,000!'

'I told you the British public love Wimbledon.'

CHAPTER 18

A FEMALE INFLUENCE

'I don't know what all the fuss is about,' Andy said to Jamie. 'She was one of the best players in the women's game in recent years, she knows how to win Grand Slams, and if there's one thing I want, it's to win more Grand Slams.'

He was speaking to his brother after announcing that France's Amélie Mauresmo would take over as his new coach in the summer of 2014. It was very rare for a woman to coach a player on the men's tour, especially someone as good as Andy, and the appointment raised plenty of eyebrows in the tennis world.

'We've always had a strong female presence in our

lives, ever since Mum started coaching us at tennis,' Andy said.

'I'm sure it will be a good move,' Jamie agreed. 'As long as Amélie doesn't tell you off like Mum used to do!'

Amélie's arrival had followed the departure of Ivan earlier in the year. He had grown tired of all the travel and training, and wanted to focus on other things.

'If I am going to be your coach, it's only right that I give you 110 per cent of my time,' Ivan explained. 'I can't do that at the moment.'

Andy was sad to see Ivan go but he understood his reasons behind the decision.

'We've won a lot and had some great times too. It's been the best two years of my tennis career.'

'Who knows? One day we might do it all again...'

The loss of Ivan was another blow in what was proving a frustrating season for Andy. Not only was he taking longer than expected to recover from his back injury, but also faced another change to his coaching team when he parted company from Dani, his trusty training partner, after five years on the road together.

It was nothing personal against his old friend, but Andy felt like it was time for a change to freshen things up. The pair had come a long way together since that first practice session back in Barcelona.

Despite the off-court upheaval, there were still plenty of strong performances on the court, including Andy reaching the semi-finals at the French Open, the Grand Slam tournament played on clay.

'There's no shame in losing to Rafa,' Kim said comfortingly after Andy's loss to the Spaniard. 'He's the king of clay.'

While Andy failed to reach the heights of 2013, with Amélie on board he finally ended his fourteen-month wait for a trophy when he beat Tommy Robredo from Spain in the Shenzhen Open final. It was his first title since Wimbledon.

'Hopefully we won't have to wait another fourteen months until the next one,' he joked to Amélie as he posed for pictures for the pack of photographers.

'Don't worry. With the schedule I've got planned

for you, there will be plenty more chances for some silverware in the next couple of months.'

That sounded good to Andy. With his back continuing to improve every day, he wanted to make up for lost time and play as much as he could. And he certainly got his wish.

In an action-packed journey from China to Paris with stops in Vienna and Valencia in between, he played a total of twenty-three matches in thirty-seven days – and snaffled two more trophies along the way.

'I'd almost forgotten what it felt like to win a trophy,' he joked to Jamie at the end of the season.

'Well, now that you're back to winning ways, hopefully you can add a few more to the collection next year. Have you got any targets for the new season?'

'Funny you should mention it. There's one tournament in particular that I've got my eye on – and I'm going to need your help to win it.'

CHAPTER 19

PRIDE OF BRITAIN

'Nice to see you again, Leon. Bit different from the wet and windy courts in Dunblane, isn't it?'

Andy was standing next to Leon Smith inside the Glasgow Emirates Arena, where later that day Great Britain would play the USA in the first round of the Davis Cup. So much had changed for both men and so many years had passed since Leon had coached Andy but now, once again, they were on the same team as player and coach.

Leon was one of the most respected coaches in the sport. He was appointed Head of Men's Tennis at the Lawn Tennis Association in 2010, the same year that he took over as Great Britain's Davis Cup captain.

And that was good news for Andy – he absolutely loved the Davis Cup.

The tournament was the tennis equivalent of the World Cup in football. Instead of player v player, it was country v country. The best players from each country would team up to take on other countries in a knockout format, played over four singles and one doubles match.

Andy loved representing his country, he loved being part of a team and he definitely loved watching the World Cup. What made it even more special was it gave him the chance to play alongside his brother.

As they looked forward to the 2015 tournament, Andy felt GB had a chance to do something spectacular.

'We've got a really strong team, Leon. In the singles, there are loads of talented players to choose from, including James Ward, Dan Evans and Kyle Edmund, plus Jamie and Dom Inglot in the doubles.'

'Don't forget to add your own name to the list!'

Andy felt Britain had the potential to go all

the way. It had been far too long since that last happened.

'Do you remember how your Wimbledon win was the first by a British man since Fred Perry in 1936?' Leon asked Andy.

'How could I forget? People reminded me of that nearly every day until I won the title.'

'Well, guess when Britain last won the Davis Cup?'

'Don't tell me…'

'Yep, you got it – 1936, with Fred Perry winning the deciding match.'

Andy laughed. The ghost of the brilliant British player Fred Perry had seemed to follow him wherever he went in his career.

A couple of hours later, a sea of blue greeted Andy as he walked into the indoor arena. All around the stadium, fans were decked out in blue for Britain. They waved GB flags, they wore GB trousers, they swapped GB hats. 'Some of them probably even wear GB pants,' Andy thought.

They also sang songs.

One Andy Murray
There's only one Andy Murray
One Andy Murraaaaaaay
There's only one Andy Murray.

It was just the kind of atmosphere that brought the best out of Andy. He rose to the occasion in his match against Donald Young to give Britain the perfect start.

After putting the first point on the board for GB, Andy could turn his attention to another favourite pastime – being his country's No. 1 cheerleader.

'Come on, Wardy!' he yelled.

Over the five sets that followed, Andy screamed, shouted, sang and fist-pumped his support from the sidelines, as Wardy staged an astonishing comeback to stun America's top-ranked player John Isner 15–13 in the final set.

'I'm exhausted just watching you, so I can't imagine how you're feeling,' he said to Wardy after the match.

The next day, Jamie and Dom came within a

whisker of beating the Bryan brothers, the best doubles players in the modern era. Andy felt sorry for his brother after such a tight loss but there was one positive from the defeat – it meant he got another chance to play in front of the Scottish crowd in the singles.

The result was never in doubt as Britain's hero saw off Isner in straight sets to seal the tie.

The quarter-final against France was played at a different venue, but that didn't stop the fans making plenty of noise at Queen's Club in London.

You are my Andy
My Andy Murray
You make me happy when skies are grey
You'll never know, pal, how much I love you
So please don't take my Andy away.

With the tie level at 1–1 going into the doubles, Leon wanted to try a different strategy.

'How are you feeling, Andy?'

'Great. I could happily play Jo-Wilfried Tsonga

again right now,' Andy replied, referring to the opponent he had already beaten that day.

'Well, that won't be necessary,' Leon smiled, 'but make sure you get a good night's sleep as I'm going to pair you up with Jamie tomorrow. Let's see how France cope with double trouble from the Murrays.'

Not very well, as it turned out. Years of playing together meant Andy always knew where Jamie was on court and had a sixth sense about what he would do next. It was a winning combination and the French pairing of Tsonga and Nicolas Mahut were powerless to stop them.

Of course, the spectators had their very own song for the brothers.

Andy
Andy, Andy
Andy, Andy
Andy, Andy Murray.

And then it was Jamie's turn.

Jamie
Jamie, Jamie
Jamie, Jamie
Jamie, Jamie Murray.

After the victory in the doubles, Andy won again in the singles to ensure Britain would play in the semi-finals for the first time in thirty-four years.

That tie against Australia was held back in Glasgow, and it followed a remarkably similar pattern. Andy won both his singles and teamed up with Jamie again in the doubles for another crucial victory.

The only difference was there was yet another new song.

We love you Andy, we do
We love you Andy, we do
We love you Andy, we do
Oh Andy, we love you.

'Come on, GB,' Andy roared as he converted his

match point against Bernard Tomic. The stadium erupted as Andy was engulfed by his teammates.

GB were going to the final!

With eight wins from eight matches, Andy was the undisputed leader of the team. And if they were going to match the achievement of their countrymen from 1936, he would need to deliver another top-notch performance in the final against Belgium.

The final would take place in Belgium itself, in Ghent, thirty-five miles outside the capital city, Brussels.

'We've been lucky to have amazing support in our first three matches, which have all been at home,' Andy said. 'Hopefully, a few of our fans will be able to make the journey over.'

There were far more than a few, and Andy heard them before he could even see them.

Let's go, GB, let's go
Let's go, GB, let's go.

Then as he walked from the tunnel into the stadium before the first match between Kyle Edmund and David Goffin, he saw thousands of those familiar blue shirts.

'It's like we're playing in Glasgow all over again,' a stunned Andy said to Leon.

A narrow defeat for Kyle was followed by a convincing win for Andy over Ruben Bemelmans. The next day, it was a no-brainer for Leon to pair Andy and Jamie together again in the doubles, and there was one very proud mother in the stands.

'Well played, boys!' Judy shouted as her sons gave Britain a 2–1 advantage to stand on the brink of history.

'This is your World Cup final,' Leon said to Andy before his final match against Goffin the following day. 'Win this one and the trophy is coming home to Britain.'

'There's nothing I want more,' Andy replied.

Andy had proved too strong for his Davis Cup opponents all year long, and he delivered another superhero performance when it mattered most.

He saved the best until the very last point of the tournament, finishing a twenty-shot rally with an exquisite backhand lob.

Great Britain were Davis Cup champions.

Just like his Wimbledon victory two years earlier, the long wait was over. Andy collapsed onto the court in disbelief. Before long he seemed to have disappeared completely – Jamie, Leon and all the team members jumped on top of him to celebrate.

As he went to bed that night, the words of the commentary from that final point were ringing in his ears.

'Great Britain have done it in the most spectacular style. Andy Murray – unbeaten in Davis Cup. More sporting history. What a point to finish. Unreal.'

CHAPTER 20

THE GRASS IS GREEN AGAIN

'So, did you miss me?' Ivan asked with a twinkle in his eye.

'Not half as much as I bet you missed me!' Andy replied, shaking his coach's hand.

'Right, enough small talk. Let's get down to business.'

Andy smiled. Same old Ivan.

Ivan had always brought a no-nonsense approach to his coaching. He told Andy exactly what he thought. If he was playing well, Ivan would praise him, and if he wasn't, he would let him know about it.

That was exactly what Andy felt he needed in the summer of 2016.

Three years had passed since his magical Wimbledon triumph and he was still waiting to add another Grand Slam trophy to his collection. There had been several near misses – including defeats in that year's Australian and French Open finals to Novak (who else?) – but near enough was not good enough for Andy. And so when the opportunity arose to get Ivan back on his coaching team, he jumped at the chance.

Much had changed in Andy's life since Ivan was last by his side. He had married Kim in 2015, choosing Dunblane Cathedral as the venue – to the delight of his mother. Then in February 2016, there had been a new addition to the Murray clan, when baby Sophia was born.

'It has made me realise that there are more important things in life than tennis,' Andy told Jamie one day. 'Win or lose, I always cheer up when I get home and see Sophia.'

'As long as you don't have to change too many nappies!' Jamie joked.

'I thought changing nappies could be part of your uncle duties!'

Andy's first tournament with Ivan on his team was the Queen's Club championship. He won the title for a record fifth time. It was like his old coach had never been away.

'Are you sure you haven't missed me?' Ivan chuckled.

Andy didn't mind the teasing one bit. With Ivan on board, he knew he had a terrific chance of winning his next tournament too, and this was the one that really mattered – Wimbledon.

Of course, Andy knew that lifting the famous Challenge Cup for a second time would be far easier said than done. Winning Wimbledon once was a momentous effort in itself – he still had dreams (or maybe nightmares) about that final tortuous game against Novak in 2013.

'Only twenty-nine men have won Wimbledon more than once in the tournament's 140-year history,' said Ivan, always on hand with a useful stat.

'Let's hope thirty is my lucky number this year,' replied Andy.

It was just like the old days as Andy prepared

for his opening match against fellow Briton Liam Broady, with Judy, Kim and Ivan all sitting together in the stands. There was no way Kim would miss her husband's matches, and baby Sophia was allowed to go in a crèche inside the grounds as Wimbledon officials made an exception to their 'no baby' rule.

'This one's for Sophia,' a delighted Andy said after easing into the second round.

His mood got even better later in the week. As he was preparing for his third-round match against Australia's John Millman, Ivan burst into the dressing room.

'Sam Querrey has done your job for you.'

'What do you mean?' asked a puzzled Andy. As usual, he was focusing on the match ahead of him, and not thinking about any other players.

'He's knocked out Novak.'

'Wow.'

Novak was the two-time defending champion and had won the last four Grand Slam tournaments. He was the undisputed world No. 1 and Andy had been certain that to win Wimbledon again, he needed to find a way to beat his old rival.

Not any more...

'That is a massive shock,' he said. 'We can't take anything for granted, though – there are still loads of great players in the draw.'

But none of them could match Andy. He was playing such mesmerising tennis – the only time he dropped any sets on his way to the final came in the quarter-final when he needed five sets to overcome Jo-Wilfried Tsonga.

As always, the boisterous British fans were there to cheer him on. And this time, when Andy reached the final against Canada's Milos Raonic, there was a different feeling among the crowd. They expected him to win.

While Andy might have been the favourite, he still knew it would be far from easy. Milos had knocked out Roger Federer in the semi-finals and boasted one of the fastest, and nastiest, serves in the world. Luckily, Andy was the best returner in the game, with reflexes as fast as a ninja – just like his hero Andre Agassi.

He had another huge advantage on his side:
experience. While this match was the Canadian's
first taste of a Grand Slam final, Andy was used
to handling the pressure of big occasions and he
showed no sign of nerves as he won the first two
sets.

'Stay calm. You're in control of the match,' he told
himself. 'Just keep doing everything you've practised
in training.'

While Andy was calm on the court, Ivan remained
as cool as ever off it; while Judy and Kim jumped in
the air after every winning shot, the coach stayed
glued to his seat.

In the third set, Milos threw everything at Andy in
a desperate bid to claw his way back into the match.
At six games all, a tiebreak was required to decide
the set – the first player to seven points would claim
the spoils. If Milos succeeded, he would be back
in contention; if it was Andy, it was game, set and
match.

Andy had given the Centre Court crowd some
heart-stopping moments over the years, but not

today. He charged into a 5–0 lead and quickly brought up four match points. Unlike three years earlier, he only needed one of them, finishing the job at the first time of asking.

At that exact moment, any traces of the cool, calm and collected Andy – who had engineered a 6–4, 7–6, 7–6 victory – vanished. Suddenly he was replaced by an ecstatic, shouting, first-pumping Andy, who threw his racket on to the grass in joy.

Wimbledon champion.

Again.

'I'm so proud to have my hands on the trophy again,' he said after the match. 'This is the most important tournament to me every year.'

The fans cheered wildly at that comment – everyone could see how much Wimbledon meant to him.

The victory meant a huge amount to Ivan, too. He had never won Wimbledon as a player, twice losing at the final hurdle. As Andy lovingly cradled the Challenge Cup, he could have sworn he spotted a tear trickling down his coach's face in the stands.

Ivan was usually so stony faced he would make a statue look emotional.

'Great to have the winning team back together, Ivan,' he said later. 'I've got to ask you – did you shed a tear when I won today?'

'Of course not. I've got really bad hay fever!'

CHAPTER 21

DANCING TO THE SAMBA BEAT

'What? Me? Really?...

...Are you serious?...

...What do you mean, "Will I do it?" Of course, I'll do it...

...I will remember it for the rest of my life...

...Thank you... thank you so much.'

The phone call ended. Andy's face was a mixture of delight and disbelief.

'I love the Olympics!' he shouted so loudly that Jamie rushed into the room.

'Are you feeling okay?'

'I'm more than okay. I have just been asked to be

Great Britain's flag-bearer at the opening ceremony of the Olympic Games. What an incredible honour.'

'Congratulations. Just think, billions of people around the world will be watching you. Make sure you don't drop the flag!' Jamie said with a chuckle.

But nothing could deflate Andy's mood. After the highs of winning gold in London in 2012, he had been so keen for the Games to come around again. Now they were finally here, in the Brazilian city of Rio de Janeiro, and he – out of all of the 366 athletes who would represent Team GB – had been chosen to carry the Union flag.

If that wasn't enough, there was the small matter of trying to become the first ever player to defend the Olympic singles title.

The Opening Ceremony was every bit as exciting as Andy had dreamed. An incredible spectacle of flashing lights, colour and Brazilians dancing as only they can to the samba beat – in front of 78,000 fans in the Maracanã Stadium.

'There are a few more spectators here than at

Centre Court,' Andy thought as he gazed around the massive venue.

Then it was his moment – the athletes' parade. The 207 teams competing in Rio took it in turns to walk into the stadium, each with their own flag-bearer. As Great Britain's name was read out by the announcer, Andy took a deep breath and led Team GB out to an almighty roar, waving the flag in the air.

'Come on, GB. Let's do our country proud.'

It was a night he would never forget.

The next morning, Andy had to put any thoughts of the ceremony to one side; he had a tennis match to think about – or two, to be precise. Just as in London, Andy was competing in the men's singles and men's doubles, as well as the mixed doubles later in the week. But the tournament got off to the worst possible start as Andy and Jamie were knocked out in the first round of the doubles.

'We gave our all out there, but it just wasn't enough,' Andy said to Jamie afterwards.

'I'm gutted that we're out, but at least I don't have to get on a plane and go to my next tournament just yet,' Jamie replied. 'We can go back and enjoy staying in the athletes' village.'

The athletes' village was yet another reason why the Olympics were so special. For two weeks, it was home to more than 10,000 athletes, from so many different countries and cultures but all with one thing in common – they were very good at sport.

Some competitors chose not to live in the village, but Andy was determined to stay there so he could soak up the amazing atmosphere and spend time with the other athletes. As soon as he entered the Team GB apartment block, he knew he had made the right choice. As well as a swimming pool, jacuzzis, table tennis and pool tables, there were deckchairs sporting the British colours, in front of a giant TV screen where the athletes could catch all the Olympic action. There were even bikes – again in the famous red, white and blue colours – which the athletes could use to cycle around the village.

The Team GB tennis team all stayed in the same apartment. For Andy, sharing a room with his brother and with Leon Smith as their coach, it was just like growing up in Dunblane.

Except for one small difference – they were surrounded by sporting superstars.

Andy loved hearing everyone's stories and experiences. He wanted to meet as many athletes as possible and quickly struck up a friendship with Justin Rose, the star golfer.

'It feels incredible to be part of a much bigger team,' he said to Justin.

However, he didn't his whole time in Rio socialising – there was also a tennis competition to win.

While his mixed doubles hopes were ended in the quarter-finals, Andy replicated his London form in the singles, winning his first five matches to set up a gold medal showdown against Argentina's Juan Martín del Potro.

One of the most popular players on the tour, Juan Martín was back to his best after a bad run of injuries. In the first round, he had produced a stunning performance to knock out Novak – despite almost missing the match after being stuck in a lift for forty minutes.

Andy knew he couldn't afford many mistakes if he was to bring home a gold medal. It had already been an unforgettable day for Team GB. While Andy waited for his final, he watched in awe as Justin won the golf tournament, Jason Kenny claimed gold on the cycling track, and Max Whitlock went one better to win two gymnastics golds.

Andy was inspired. 'Come on, let's add another gold to Team GB's tally,' he said to himself.

The final was more like a war than a tennis match. The two players threw everything at each other over an exhausting four hours. And the crowd loved every second of it.

Thousands of fans from Argentina had travelled up to Rio to cheer on their hero. Andy, meanwhile, had the support of the Brazilian locals.

'*Vamos Juan Martin!*' the Argentinians bellowed when Juan Martin won a point.

'*Ole, ole, ole, ole!*' the Brazilians responded when Andy won the next point.

The lead changed hands several times in a see-sawing encounter, but eventually it was Andy who came out on top, edging out his opponent in four gruelling sets.

He had done what no man before him had managed to achieve – he had defended his Olympic title.

At the end, the two warriors hugged at the net, almost too tired to speak.

'I'm sorry there could only be one winner today, Juan Martín. You played like a champion.'

'Thanks Andy. It was such a tough match,' Juan Martín replied, still holding his opponent. 'If I let go of you, I think I might fall over!'

Back at the apartment block that evening, Andy and Justin proudly showed off their gold medals to each other.

'What a great experience,' Justin said. 'Bring on the Tokyo Olympics in 2020. Will I see you there?

'I'll be thirty-three, four years older, and maybe four years slower,' Andy replied, 'but nothing could stop me from being there. I love the Olympics.'

CHAPTER 22

NUMBERS GAME

'World number one – it's got a nice ring to it, hasn't it?'

'It'll never happen this year, Ivan. It's too big a gap.'

'Don't be so sure. You've almost halved the gap in the last three months alone.'

'But to have a chance I'll need to win my next five tournaments.'

'Then we'd better stop all this talking and start practising.'

Andy smiled at his coach. Nothing was impossible in Ivan's world – even wrestling the world No. 1 spot off Novak, which he had held for 122 weeks.

That was his new target for 2016.

Andy had never topped the world rankings but, after enjoying his best ever season on tour, he now had an outside chance. It would be the perfect way to end an incredible year, but he could not afford a single mistake.

The ATP World Tour rankings are based on numbers. The better you perform and the more tournaments you win, the more points you get. At the start of 2016, Novak had led Andy by almost 8,000 points – an enormous advantage. By April, his old rival had increased his lead to 8,725. Yet by the end of the summer, after Andy's triumphs at Wimbledon and the Olympics, the gap between them was narrowing.

'Did you know that a British player has never held the number-one spot since computerised rankings began back in 1973?' Ivan said, rolling out another stat.

'Really? Well, I'm not surprised they needed a computer to work out all these numbers,' Andy replied. 'I'm getting a sore head just from looking at them.'

Andy always loved to push himself and he set about his latest challenge with relish. First up was the China Open in Beijing at the start of October, a tournament he simply had to win to give himself any chance.

It couldn't have gone any better – five matches played, five matches won, without losing a set.

Ivan was on hand to offer plenty of encouragement afterwards.

'I told you that you could do this, Andy. Let's just take it one tournament at a time and see how Novak handles the pressure.'

His next tournament, the Shanghai Masters, was a carbon copy of the previous week. Five more wins, each with the minimum of fuss.

'You're reeling Novak in, Andy. He knows you're coming for him.'

While Andy picked up two trophies in as many weeks, Novak was struggling for form, not helped by injuries to his wrist and elbow. The points deficit that had been over 8,000 in June was now only 2,415.

Next up for Andy was the Erste Bank Open in

Vienna. It might have been a tournament on a
different continent, but it was the same result as
he reeled off another five wins to get within 2,000
points of the top spot.

'He can feel you breathing down his neck. You've
almost got him,' Ivan said afterwards.

Andy's incredible run of form – 15 wins from 15
– meant that he could claim the No. 1 ranking at the
next event in Paris. Once again, though, he would
need a perfect week, and hope that Novak failed to
make the final.

To make things even tougher, Andy was running
out of steam. The only downside to winning so many
tournaments was there was little time to relax in
between competitions. Week after week after week.
He needed a rest. But there was no way he was
going to put his feet up now; he was so close to the
world No. 1 spot he could almost touch it.

For Paris, read Beijing, Shanghai and Vienna
beforehand – Andy eased through the draw to book a
semi-final clash with Milos Raonic.

The pressure was too much for Novak. In his

quarter-final against Marin Čilić, he cracked, losing to the Croat for the first time in fifteen matches.

That result opened the door for Andy to climb to the summit of world tennis. All he had to do was beat Milos.

After such a tough battle to get to this point, the final blow couldn't have been easier. Milos was forced to withdraw due to injury, meaning Andy had become the new world No. 1 without even picking up his racket.

'Congratulations,' Ivan said. 'You are now – officially – the best player in the world. Not that I ever had any doubt!'

Andy beamed. World No. 1. He couldn't believe it. It had been such an eventful journey from when he first started playing in Dunblane twenty-six years earlier.

'I never thought I'd be number one,' he said. 'This isn't something that's happened over the last few weeks or months. It's taken years and years of work to get here – with a lot of help from lots of people.'

Cementing his newfound status, Andy quickly

wrapped up the Paris final, then defeated Novak
to win the season-ending tournament in London.
In barely six weeks, he had recorded twenty-five
victories in a row, to win five tournaments – just as
Ivan had said he would. Having at one point trailed
Novak by nearly 9,000 ranking points, he now held a
905-point advantage.

No one else came close to the pair of them,
with nearest rivals Milos, Stan Wawrinka and Kei
Nishikori more than 6,000 points adrift. Andy and
Novak were in a different class from the rest of the
field, and – for the first time – Andy was looking
down on all of them.

CHAPTER 23

ARISE SIR ANDY

What a season.

Even by Andy's high standards, 2016 had been mind-blowingly successful. He had won nine titles, including Wimbledon and Olympic gold in Rio. He was the world No. 1 and he had been voted the BBC Sports Personality of the Year for a record third time.

While he never expected to have such an incredible year, Andy had always believed that success would come if he kept working hard and kept performing to his best.

But there was one final honour in 2016 that caught him completely by surprise. It didn't come on the tennis court, but by email.

Andy woke up one morning at his training camp in Miami and checked his emails on his phone. A message from Buckingham Palace immediately caught his eye.

'You have been chosen to be a Knight of the Order of the British Empire…'

Andy stopped reading and rubbed his eyes. 'Am I still dreaming?'

He read the message again.

There it was in black and white – he had been officially recognised with a knighthood for services to tennis and charity.

He shook his head in disbelief. Only the absolute greats of British sport held knighthoods – the likes of Sir Steve Redgrave, Sir Alex Ferguson, Sir Chris Hoy. Now, he was about to join them. Andy Murray from Dunblane was going to be Sir Andy Murray.

He shook his head some more. What an honour.

Andy was desperate to tell his coaching team in Miami and his mates back home, but he wasn't allowed. The Buckingham Palace rules insisted that he couldn't say anything until the Queen's New Year Honours List was announced at the end of December.

Andy made sure his knighthood remained a secret, although he couldn't keep the news from his closest family – he didn't think the Queen would mind!

'Well done, Andy,' Judy said. 'You deserve it – both for your tennis achievements and all the charity work you do.'

'We're so proud of you,' said Kim.

'We are not worthy,' Jamie joked, kneeling down in front of Andy. 'Did you know you're the youngest person ever to be knighted and the first tennis player to become a Sir while still playing?'

Andy did not know. It was yet another surprise.

However, while he was very excited about the honour, he did have one concern. He was worried that the knighthood might distract him and affect his performances on the court. He didn't want to make a big song and dance about his new status.

So when some of his fellow players came up to him at the start of the new season and asked what they should call him, he replied humbly: 'Andy is fine, thanks.'

There was still so much more he wanted to achieve – and he didn't want anything to get in his way. Another Wimbledon title, more Grand Slam trophies, keeping Novak off the No. 1 spot, possibly even a third Olympic gold – they were all targets for the months and years ahead.

Andy always wanted to push himself further. He was never satisfied and was determined to keep improving – and that's what made him Britain's greatest ever tennis player.

ANDY MURRAY HONOURS

Wimbledon
★ 2013, 2016

US Open
★ 2012

Olympic Games
★ Singles: gold (2012, 2016)
★ Mixcd doubles: silver (2012)

ATP World Tour Finals
★ 2016

Davis Cup
★ 2015

Highest world ranking
★ 1 (November 2016)

ITF World Champion
★ 2016

BBC Sports Personality of the Year
★ 2013, 2015, 2016

Turn the page for a sneak preview
of another brilliant sporting story by. . .
John Murray

CHRIS FROOME

Available now!

978 1 78606 466 0

CHAPTER 1

KING OF FRANCE

One hundred and thirteen kilometres to go. That was all that stood between him and victory. The equivalent of riding from London to Southampton. A tough task for any ordinary cyclist, but not for someone who had already ridden more than 3,000 km in the previous three weeks – and that included pedalling up some of the highest mountains in Europe.

Chris smiled and waved to the cheering crowd as he set off from the start line. The sun was out, there was a party atmosphere, and he was going to enjoy each and every one of the 113 km facing him.

The fans screamed their support.

'Go on, Chris.'

'Well done, Froomey.'

'Bring the yellow jersey home for Britain!'

It was the twenty-first and final stage of the 2016 Tour de France, the most famous and most challenging bike race in the whole world, and Chris was on the verge of winning it for the third time. Only seven men in the race's 103-year history had done that before.

While there was still one stage to go, it was tradition that the final leg of the Tour was a procession, where riders would not attack or try to gain time on the race leader. If Chris could stay on his bike, he would win the Tour. His smile grew even bigger when that thought crossed his mind.

As the race leader, Chris wore the yellow jersey – or *maillot jaune*, as the French fans called it – instead of the usual blue of Team Sky. That made it very easy for other riders to spot him.

'You deserve it, mate,' said his former teammate, Australia's Richie Porte, patting him on the back.

'Congratulations, Chris. You were too strong for us this year… but I'll be even stronger next year,' chuckled Romain Bardet, the French cyclist who was second in the overall rankings.

'Thanks, Romain,' Chris laughed. 'I was hoping you might go easy on me!'

It made a pleasant change to have a friendly conversation with his rivals. Chris had spent three weeks locked in a deadly battle with them around the roads of France in his bid to win the Tour. Every day, they had been his enemies.

There had been some unforgettable moments along the mammoth journey, including his daredevil descent down a mountain to win Stage 8 and a thrilling attack during a windy Stage 11 to gain some more precious seconds. There were other moments Chris would have preferred to forget, such as when he crashed on Stage 19 and had to use his teammate Geraint Thomas's bike to get to the finish.

'It was definitely worth all the pain,' Chris said to himself, as he gaped open-mouthed at the thousands upon thousands of fans standing at the side of the road. He could never believe that so many people would come to watch them race. It was one of the things that made the Tour de France extra special.

As he pedalled along, Chris started thinking about how far he had come from the days growing up in Kenya, when he used to ride his old supermarket bike in the hills, looking down on the stunning African landscape, day after day, for hours on end. Back then, who could have imagined that he would become a three-time Tour de France champion?

'Wake up, Froomey. We're coming up to the Champs-Élysées.'

Chris was snapped back to reality by Geraint's voice – or G as the Welsh rider was known by everyone at Team Sky. 'There's still some work to do before we start the celebrations.'

'Sorry, G!'

While much of the final stage was ridden at a gentle pace, the race began in earnest when the riders arrived at the Champs-Élysées. Nine times they would lap around the famous avenue in the centre of Paris, travelling at breakneck speed. Just one mistake here, one crash, and Chris's dream of glory could be ruined.

'Keep your concentration,' Chris said to himself as he cycled past the Arc de Triomphe monument. 'One big last push.'

Chris was surrounded by his Sky teammates. They had played a huge part in his victory, protecting their leader from other riders, chasing down his rivals, and giving him food and drink – or, in G's case, his bike!

The team weren't bothered about winning the individual stage today; all that mattered was making sure Chris reached the finish line safely. He held a four-minute advantage over Romain, so had plenty of time to spare.

As the sprinters tore up the Champs-Élysées one last time, with André Greipel crossing the line first, Team Sky stayed well out of trouble at the back of the main group of cyclists.

With the finish in sight, Chris called out to his teammates.

'Come on, boys. Let's finish this together. This is a victory for our whole team as much as for me. I couldn't have done it without you.'

And with that, the nine cyclists from Team Sky linked arms and rode to the finish in one single line.

Chris had done it. After an exhausting eighty-nine hours in the saddle, he was the Tour de France champion!

He had previously won the Tour in 2013 and 2015 and now he had become the first cyclist in twenty years to retain his title. What an incredible achievement.

'This is the best day of my life,' Chris said after the race, dedicating the victory to his wife Michelle and to his seven-month-old son Kellan, who was there to watch his father win. 'It's an absolutely amazing feeling. To wear the yellow jersey is every cyclist's dream.'

CATCH UP WITH THE BRILLIANT FOOTBALL HEROES SERIES

RONALDO

MESSI

The Rocket tells of how Cristiano Ronaldo overcame poverty and childhood illness to become one of the best football players ever. Escaping the hot streets of Madeira, Ronaldo first proved himself as a wonder-kid at Manchester United under Sir Alex Ferguson, before becoming a legend for Real Madrid and Portugal. This is the story of how the gifted boy became a man, a team-player and a legend.

Lionel Messi is a legend – Barcelona's star player and the world's best footballer. But when was young, he was so small that his friends would call him 'Little Leo' and coaches worried he wasn't big enough to play. Yet through bravery, talent and hard work, he proved them all wrong. Little Lion tells the magical story of how the tiniest boy in South America grew up to become the greatest player on earth.

978 1 78606 405 9
£5.99

978 1 78606 379 3
£5.99

COLLECT THEM ALL

NEYMAR

POGBA

Neymar da Silva Santos Júnior is the boy with the big smile who carries the hopes of Brazil on his shoulders. Neymar now stands alongside Pelé and Ronaldinho as a Brazilian footballing hero. Bidding a fond farewell to his home in São Paolo, Neymar's dreams finally came true when he joined Barcelona. Now, alongside Messi and Suárez, he is part of the most feared attacking trident in the game. This is the heart-warming true story of Neymar's road to glory.

978 1 78606 379 3
£5.99

Paul Pogba: Pogboom tells the exciting story of how French wonder-kid Paul Pogba became Europe's best young player, and finally fulfilled his dream of returning to his boyhood club Manchester United in a world-record transfer. The sky is the limit for United's new star.

978 1 78606 379 3
£5.99

COLLECT THEM ALL

INIESTA

GIGGS

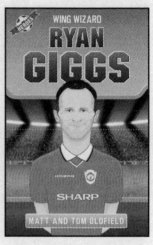

Andrés was always smaller than his friends, but he refused to let that stop him becoming one of the most special footballers of all time. *Andrés Iniesta: The Illusionist* tells of how his talent and hard work shone through as he rose through the ranks to become captain of the greatest Barcelona side ever, and scored the winning goal in the World Cup final for Spain.

978 1 78606 380 9
£5.99

Ryan Giggs: Wing Wizard is the classic story of one of Manchester United's all-time heroes. As a teenager, he was so brilliant that Sir Alex Ferguson turned up at his front door to sign him – and the rest is history. A dazzlingly skilful winger, and one of the most decorated players ever, Ryan Giggs is a true Premier League legend.

978 1 78606 378 6
£5.99

COLLECT THEM ALL

AGÜERO

GERRARD

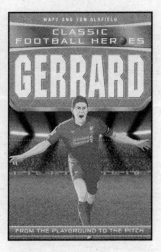

The Little Genius is the tale of the boy who would go on to change football history forever. Agüero's dramatic ninety-fourth-minute goal on the final day of the 2012/13 season, to snatch the title from under rivals Manchester United's noses, was the most electric moment in Premier League history. This is how the small boy from Argentina became the biggest hero of all.

978 1 78606 218 5
£5.99

Steven Gerrard: Captain Fantastic tells of how a young boy from Merseyside overcame personal tragedy in the Hillsborough disaster to make his dream of playing for Liverpool FC come true. But that boy was no ordinary footballer; he would go on to captain his club for over a decade, inspiring their legendary Champions League FA Cup wins along the way. This is the story of Steven Gerrard, Liverpool's greatest ever player.

978 1 78606 219 2
£5.99

COLLECT THEM ALL

IBRAHIMOVIĆ

SÁNCHEZ

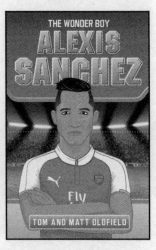

Zlatan Ibrahimović: Red Devil follows the Swedish superstar on his amazing journey from the tough streets of Malmö to becoming the deadly striker at Manchester United. Along the way he has been a star for Juventus, Inter Milan, Barcelona, and Paris Saint-Germain, as well as becoming Sweden's all-time leading goalscorer. This is the story of one of a generation's finest footballers.

978 1 78606 217 8
£5.99

Alexis Sánchez: The Wonder Boy tells the story of the Arsenal superstar's incredible journey from the streets of Tocopilla to become 'The Boy Wonder', a national hero, and one of the most talented players in the world. With his pace, skill and eye for a goal, Alexis is now one of the Premier League's biggest stars. The story is every bit as exciting as the player.

978 1 78606 013 6
£5.99

COLLECT THEM ALL

SUAREZ

HAZARD

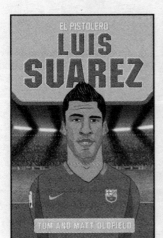

Luis Suárez: El Pistolero follows the Uruguayan's winding path from love-struck youngster to Liverpool hero to Barcelona star. Grabbing goals and headlines along the way, Luis chased his dreams and became a Champions League winner. This is the inspiring story of how the world's deadliest striker made his mark.

978 1 786060129
£5.99

Eden Hazard: The Boy in Blue is the thrilling tale of how the wing wizard went from local wonder kid to league champion. With the support of his football-obsessed family, Eden worked hard to develop his amazing dribbling skills and earn his dream transfer to Chelsea.

978 1 78606 014 3
£5.99

COLLECT THEM ALL

BALE

ROONEY

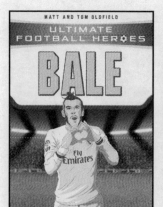

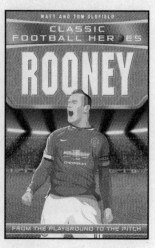

Gareth Bale: The Boy Who Became a Galáctico tracks the Welsh wizard's impressive rise from talented schoolboy to Real Madrid star. This is the inspiring story of how Bale beat the odds to become the most expensive player in football history.

978 1 78418 645 7
£5.99

Wayne Rooney: Captain of England tells the action-packed story of one boy's journey from the streets of Croxteth to one of the biggest stages in world football. This heart-warming book tracks Rooney's fairy-tale rise from child superstar to Everton hero to Manchester United legend.

978 1 78418 647 0
£5.99